Babies and Young Children in Care

Child Welfare Outcomes

Series Editor: Harriet Ward, Centre for Child and Family Research, Loughborough University, UK

This authoritative series draws from original research and current policy debates to help social work managers, policy makers and researchers to understand and improve the outcomes of services for children and young people in need. Taking an evidence-based approach, these books include children's experiences and analysis of costs and effectiveness in their assessment of interventions, and provide guidance on how to develop more effective policy, practice and training.

also in the series

Safeguarding and Promoting the Well-being of Children, Families and Communities
Edited by Jane Scott and Harriet Ward
Foreword by Maria Eagle MP
ISBN 1 84310 141 6

of related interest

Approaches to Needs Assessment in Children's Services
Edited by Harriet Ward and Wendy Rose
Foreword by Professor Al Aynsley Green
ISBN 1 85302 780 4

Foster Placements
Why They Succeed and Why They Fail
Ian Sinclair, Kate Wilson and Ian Gibbs
ISBN 1 84310 173 4

Fostering Now
Messages from Research
Ian Sinclair
Foreword by Tom Jeffreys
ISBN 1 84310 362 1

Fostering Adolescents
Elaine Farmer, Sue Moyers and Jo Lipscombe
ISBN 1 84310 227 7

Foster Carers
Why They Stay and Why They Leave
Ian Sinclair, Ian Gibbs and Kate Wilson
ISBN 1 84310 172 6

Foster Children
Where They Go and How They Get On
Ian Sinclair, Claire Baker, Kate Wilson and Ian Gibbs
ISBN 1 84310 278 1

Enhancing the Well-being of Children and Families through Effective Interventions
International Evidence for Practice
Edited by Colette McAuley, Peter Pecora and Wendy Rose
Foreword by Maria Eagle MP
ISBN 1 84310 116 5

The Developing World of the Child
Edited by Jane Aldgate, David Jones, Wendy Rose and Carole Jeffery
Foreword by Maria Eagle MP
ISBN 1 84310 244 7

Babies and Young Children in Care

Life Pathways, Decision-making and Practice

*Harriet Ward, Emily R. Munro
and Chris Dearden*

Jessica Kingsley Publishers
London and Philadelphia

First published in 2006
by Jessica Kingsley Publishers
116 Pentonville Road
London N1 9JB, UK
and
400 Market Street, Suite 400
Philadelphia, PA 19106, USA

www.jkp.com

Library of Congress Cataloging in Publication Data

Ward, Harriet, 1948-
    Babies and young children in care : life pathways, decision-making and practice / Harriet Ward, Emily
Munro and Chris Dearden.
        p. cm.
    Includes bibliographical references and index.
    ISBN-13: 978-1-84310-272-4 (hardback)
    ISBN-10: 1-84310-272-2 (hardback)
    1. Children—Institutional care—England. 2. Infants—Institutional care—England. 3. Infants—Devel-
opment—England. I. Munro, Emily, 1978- II. Dearden, Chris, 1957- III. Title.
    HV866.G7W37 2006
    362.73'208320941—dc22
                                                                                    2005037210

British Library Cataloguing in Publication Data
A CIP catalogue record for this book is available from the British Library

ISBN-13: 978 1 84310 272 4
ISBN-10: 1 84310 272 2

Printed and bound in Great Britain by
Athenaeum Press, Gateshead, Tyne and Wear

Contents

List of Figures

List of Tables

Preface

This is the second in a series of books on Child Welfare Outcomes, commissioned by Jessica Kingsley Publishers and edited by Harriet Ward. The books are primarily written for academics, researchers, policy makers and professionals concerned with improving outcomes for vulnerable children by promoting and safeguarding their well-being and that of their families.

Perhaps the most vulnerable of all children in Western societies today are very young children at risk of significant harm. This book explores the experiences of a group of 42 babies who were looked after for at least a year by six local authorities in England; it examines the relationship between their family circumstances, their life pathways and the different factors which influenced the decisions made by parents, relatives and professionals.

Inevitably the production of a book such as this relies on a number of people. The authors owe a particular debt to Don Nicholson, who advised on some of the interview schedules and assisted with the fieldwork, and to Mike Gatehouse who developed the database on which much of the analysis of research findings relied.

The study that forms the main focus of this book was funded by the Department of Health. Throughout the project we have benefited from the wise counsel and expertise provided by our liaison officers Carolyn Davies and Caroline Thomas and by our advisory group: Carole Bell, Roger Bullock, Jonathan Corbett, Janet Grauberg, Helen Jones, David Quinton, John Rowlands, Marjorie Smith and Helen Steele.

We also greatly appreciate the research assistance and advice of Sarah Lawrie, Alison Wynn, Joe Sempik, Tricia Skuse and Ian Macdonald. The book would never have been completed without the administrative support of Suzanne Dexter and Sophie Astwood. We are also grateful for the advice and help offered by our editors at Jessica Kingsley Publishers, Amy Lankester-Owen and Stephen Jones.

Our thanks must also go to the managers and liaison officers in the six participating local authorities who, for reasons of confidentiality, we cannot name. Many of them participated in our benchmarking group, which provided invaluable advice and guidance throughout the course of the study. Our greatest debt is to the professionals, birth parents and current carers who participated in the interviews, and who helped us understand more about the complex and difficult decisions that had to be made to safeguard the well-being of these very vulnerable children.

Authors' Note

Some of the terminology that was current while the babies who form the focus of this book were looked after by local authorities is now in the process of changing. Following the introduction of the Children Act 2004, all local authorities in England are required to appoint a director of children's services, who will be professionally accountable for the delivery of the authorities' education and social services functions for children, and any health functions for children delegated by an NHS body. Although the Act allows authorities flexibility over their organisational arrangements, nevertheless, the aim is to develop integrated children's services departments, responsible for the delivery of a wide range of services for children and families, and working towards the same outcomes. At the time of writing, children's services departments were coming into being, but the babies were looked after by local authority social services, and for the sake of consistency we have retained the earlier terminology throughout.

Chapter 1

Introduction, Background and Methodology

Introduction

What are the outcomes of placing children in the care of the state? Does the experience promote or inhibit their chances of achieving long-term well-being in adulthood, and in what ways? Who benefits from being placed in care or accommodation, and who does not? Are there particular issues to be confronted when children are very young? How can practitioners and social care managers use the information that they gather in the course of their work to gain more understanding of the outcomes of their services and identify where improvements can be made?

This book seeks to explore these questions. It focuses on 42 babies who entered care or accommodation in six English local authorities before their first birthday, and who were still looked after 12–24 months later. We traced their life pathways from birth until they were five or six years old.

The experiences of these very young children can best be understood against the background of the legal and policy framework in operation at the time they were looked after by local authorities, and the research evidence that identifies the needs of such children and evaluates the appropriateness of service responses. Although there have been some changes in England and Wales since the babies were first looked after, almost all the issues raised in this book remain extremely pertinent. Similarly, although the study was undertaken in England, nevertheless, evidence from other countries, including much of Western Europe, North America, Australia and New Zealand, suggests that many of the messages have relevance in other contexts and other jurisdictions (see for instance Budgell *et al.* in press; Cousins *et al.* 2003; Schulman and Behrman 1993; Selwyn and Sturgess 2001).

Policies to promote the upbringing of children with their families

The legal framework underpinning child welfare in England and Wales when these 42 babies entered the care system was, and still is, the Children Act 1989. The underlying philosophy of the Act is that it is generally best for children to be brought up by their own families. Several principles are incorporated into the legislation; of primary importance is the precept that when a court determines any question with respect to their upbringing, the welfare of the child shall be the paramount consideration (Section 1(1)). The detrimental impact of delay in proceedings is also acknowledged (Section 1(3)). However, in promoting minimal intervention in family life the 'no order principle' and the 'partnership principle' are also of importance. These specify that no court order should be made unless it benefits the child (Section 1(5)) and that practitioners should work in partnership with parents. In practice, as the experiences of these babies will show, some of these principles can be very finely balanced, and social workers may concentrate on one at the expense of another. Balancing the need to ensure that, wherever possible, children should be brought up by their parents, who may be labouring under extensive difficulties, while at the same time ensuring that the best interests of the child are kept at the heart of decision-making, is far from straightforward; working in partnership with parents who often perceive, with reason, that the power relationship is weighted against them, is by no means simple. Over half the babies in the study described in the following pages were not reunited with their families, despite exhaustive efforts by social work practitioners to work with birth parents to promote rehabilitation.

The principle that children are best cared for within their families is enshrined in the United Nations Convention on the Rights of the Child and the European Convention on Human Rights. In the United Kingdom this has been reinforced more recently by the Human Rights Act 1998, which incorporates the European Convention into British law, and was implemented in October 2000. In the context of decisions relating to child welfare, perhaps the most important rights are: 'that no one shall be subjected to inhuman or degrading treatment' (Article 3) and the right to 'respect for private and family life' (Article 8). Where there are concerns that a child may be abused, tensions may exist between these rights, as Williams (2004) points out:

> The right of the child to a family life under Article 8 may, in an abusive family, be in direct conflict with the state's positive duty to protect him or her from inhuman or degrading treatment. (p.44)

Both parents and children have a 'right to respect for private and family life', but clearly in these cases a fine balance must be struck between the rights and interests of the child and those of his or her parents. The issue is further complicated by Section 6 of the Act, which lays on public authorities a legal duty 'not to act in a way that is incompatible with a Convention Right', and Article 6 (right to a fair trial). Both of these provisions have led to concerns that parents may challenge applications for care orders or freeing orders by claiming that local authorities have contravened rights that are protected by legislation (see Family Justice Council 2004; Williams 2001). As the experiences of the children studied demonstrate, such concerns add to the complexity of decision-making in child welfare cases, and may well lead to delays in taking decisive action to remove children from dangerous or damaging situations.

Outcomes of care and accommodation

Policies to promote the upbringing of children by their families wherever possible are further reinforced by increasing concerns about the outcomes of local authority care. In spite of spiralling costs, developmental outcomes are still notoriously poor: children and young people who spend a year or more placed in care or accommodation are 11 times as likely as their peers to reach school leaving age with no qualifications, and three times as likely to have committed an offence in the previous year (Department for Education and Skills 2005a). About a quarter of the prison population have previously been looked after by a local authority, as have between a quarter and a third of rough sleepers (Social Exclusion Unit 2003). Similar outcomes have also been noted in other countries such as the USA (Courtney *et al.* 2001), Denmark (Christoffersen 1996) and the Netherlands (Jansen *et al.* 1996). However, almost all children who enter the care system have had damaging experiences before becoming looked after. Until adequate baseline data are collected we cannot identify whether poor outcomes should be attributed to the care system *per se* or to its inability to compensate adequately for previous deficits.

Although poor outcomes are unlikely to be entirely attributable to local authority care in itself, there are, nevertheless, a number of inherent problems within the system which undoubtedly exacerbate the vulnerability of some looked after children. Since the 1980s concerns have increasingly been raised regarding the frequency with which many children in care or accommodation move from one placement to another, without achieving sufficient stability to allow them to feel an accepted member of a foster family, a school or a neighbourhood. The likely consequences of such instability for children's long-term development have been documented elsewhere (Jackson and Thomas 1999; Ward 2004); in Britain, as well as in other countries, improving the stability of placements is regarded as one of the major issues to be addressed by both national and local policy and practice (Choice Protects 2003; Department of Health 1998b, 1999a; Robbins 1999, 2000, 2001; Selwyn and Sturgess 2001).

Instability of placements

Although a number of moves are necessitated because placements disrupt, it is becoming increasingly evident that a high degree of instability is built into the care system, as a large number of children are initially placed with temporary carers, pending a more appropriate placement (see Jackson and Thomas 1999; Ward and Skuse 2001). The 42 babies were drawn from a larger group of children looked after by six English local authorities, whose needs, experiences and progress we studied for four years (see Skuse, Macdonald and Ward 2001; Skuse and Ward 2003; Ward and Skuse 1999; Ward *et al.* forthcoming a). This larger group of 242 children and young people experienced 246 moves in the first year that they were looked after; 47 (19%) of these moves were because the placement broke down at the carer's request, while 133 (54%) were categorised as 'planned transitions' (Ward and Skuse 2001).

Disruptions are upsetting for all concerned, and generally bring with them feelings of disappointment and failure. In many social services departments they are also followed by a formal process of enquiry and explanation. There are, therefore, perverse incentives to categorise disruptions as 'planned transitions', particularly if a few days' notice is given before the placement terminates. Nevertheless these would only account for a proportion of planned moves; the majority are likely to be engendered by a combination of a chronic shortage of foster carers and delayed decision-making.

The shortage of foster carers is partly the result of wider social change, such as the increase in the number of women working, which has reduced the pool of available people from which to recruit (Sinclair, Wilson and Gibbs 2004). However the nature of the fostering task has also changed. A substantial reduction in the use of residential care accompanied by a rise in the proportion of adolescents looked after by local authorities, especially on a long-term basis, over the last two decades (Minty 1999) have increased the demand for foster carers and placed pressure on an already overburdened system. Changes in the needs of the looked after population have also meant that carers are increasingly expected to possess the skills necessary to care for children with complex emotional and behavioural difficulties or health problems. The requirement that carers will work in partnership with parents who can be hostile or intrusive has also added to the complexity of their task (Poirier, Chamberland and Ward forthcoming).

Local authorities have not always met these changes by commensurate increases in remuneration or recognition of the increasingly professional service required of foster carers, and many carers have chosen to work for private or voluntary agencies, which offer better employment conditions. There is a widespread perception that agency placements are more expensive than those offered by local authorities, although the absence of comparable unit costs makes this claim impossible to assess. It is, however, clear that several authorities have found it harder to replace carers who have left their service, with the result that many are facing a shortage of 'in-house' placements. The perception that agency placements are expensive has led to a reluctance to use them for all but the children with exceptionally high needs. Added to these pressures is evidence that children coming into care are staying for longer periods, causing further stress on an already overloaded system. A report by the Social Services Inspectorate (SSI) written about a year after the 42 babies became looked after revealed that social services departments were struggling with restricted placement resources and lack of placement choice (Department of Health 1998a).

Such pressures have added a further incentive to delay the decision to place children away from home for as long as possible, with the result that many enter care on an unplanned, emergency basis and later have to move to more appropriate placements. The SSI found that, in authorities assessed in safety inspections, 90 per cent of placements were unplanned (Department of Health 1998a). Further evidence of the frequency of emergency placements was found by Waterhouse and Brocklesbury (1999) whose study showed that 75 per cent of placements were crisis-led and unplanned.

The emphasis on promoting the upbringing of children by their families has meant that the service is increasingly focused on providing short-term placements for children who will quickly be reunited (Minty 1999; Ward and Skuse 2001); this assumption can further reinforce the pattern of instability, particularly if there is insufficient planning at both a strategic and an individual level. Over a third (39%) of care episodes last for less than six months (Department for Education and Skills 2005b, p.37) after which most children do return home. However, the average length of stay is increasing (Department for Education and Skills 2005b, p.10) and those children who cannot go home may initially have been placed with carers who are only registered as short-term providers, and may later be required to move to a more permanent arrangement.

Factors similar to those discussed above also underlie an increase in the numbers of children who move in and out of care, returning home to situations that eventually prove unviable, a further issue that leads to instability.

The rate of readmission in England has doubled since the 1980s (Packman and Hall 1998), and remains high. One in three (33%) of the 242 children in the wider study from which the 42 babies were drawn had been looked after at least once before the current care episode, and more than one in eight (12%) had experienced at least two previous admissions (Ward and Skuse 2001).

Decision-making and delay

One of the most difficult decisions a social worker has to make is whether to leave children with birth parents or other relatives who are finding it difficult to meet their needs or to separate them and place them with substitute carers, perhaps permanently. Separating children by placing them in care or accommodation can cause permanent harm and can only be justified if such a decision is manifestly shown to promote their long-term well-being; on the other hand, leaving children with birth parents whose parenting capacity is diminished by multiple, and possibly long-term, difficulties can, potentially, be more damaging, particularly if effective and timely family support services are in short supply.

The pressures to promote the upbringing of children with their families, together with the incentives to reduce the number of children in care and restrict their length of stay, are likely to have made it harder for practitioners to recognise that a small number of birth families will not be able to provide good enough parenting within a child's timescale and their children will need permanent placements away from home. For many years now there have been concerns that children who could not safely return home drifted in care, without realistic long-term plans to secure their future (see Rowe and Lambert 1973). In England and Wales, both the Children Act 1975 and the Children Act 1989 intended to address such concerns, but there is still evidence that drift and delay persist (Department of Health 2000a). As Chapters 2, 3 and 4 show, concerns about instability and delay are corroborated by the experiences of the 42 babies we studied.

The purpose of exploring the life pathways of these babies in some detail was to add to the knowledge base that can inform such decisions, for the current lack of sufficient evidence increases the complexity of the prac-titioner's task:

> Social work decisions are often problematic balancing acts, based on incomplete information, within time constraints, under pressure from different sources, with uncertainty as to the likely outcome of different decisions. (O'Sullivan 1999, p.3)

Reder and Duncan (1999) found that practitioners can become overwhelmed with the possible consequences of taking action, resulting in 'assessment paralysis'. They may, for example, feel they have insufficient information to make a decision, and as a result prolong the assessment process. Similarly, Beckett (2001) suggests that there is a "psychological gradient" in the direction of delay, since postponing a decision may frequently be the line of least resistance' (cited in Beckett and McKeigue 2003, p.37). One of the most important messages from the study on which this book focuses is that postponing a decision is a decision in itself, and may well prove detrimental to a child's long-term well-being.

Although the Children Act 1989 incorporated the principle that drift and delay were detrimental (Section 11), in practice it has proved difficult to reduce them, not only in social work decision-making, but also in the actions of the courts (Hunt 1998). Wall (1997) suggests that the courts' confirmation of the importance of rehabilitation has served to delay stability and security for those children who are in need of permanent placement away from home. As Chapter 4 demonstrates, such delays are engendered by the different perspectives held by social services, the courts and birth parents. Court *processes* have also been found to cause delays (Beckett 2000, 2001; Beckett and McKeigue 2003; Hunt 1998). The time taken to conclude court proceedings has increased year on year since the implementation of the Children Act 1989 (Beckett 2001). In the context of children's timescales, Beckett (2000) describes such delays as a form of 'system abuse'.

Delays in young children achieving permanence can also be caused by long waits before their *parents* receive support. There would appear to be a mismatch between adult and children's services in the sense that adult services rarely take into account the need for speed in addressing parents' problems where there is an impact on the children in a family. For example, parents who need support services to address substance or alcohol abuse are likely to wait a considerable time, as places on rehabilitation programmes are scarce. If a child cannot in the meantime live with a substance or alcohol misusing parent, then any delay for the adult has a knock-on effect on the child. Aldridge and Becker (2003) found evidence of similar delays for adults awaiting and receiving mental health support, and these also had a negative impact on some of their children. Moreover, children's timeframes tend to be much shorter than those of adults: 'six weeks is a very long time in the experience of a six-week-old baby' (Cooper and Webb 1999, p.121).

The problem of adult and children's services not sharing information and working together has been widely documented (Laming 2003). Some of the policy developments outlined below reflect increasing recognition of the need for exchange of information and closer cooperation and joint working. This would appear to be essential where very young children are concerned, as the longer they remain looked after the less chance there is of successful reunification with birth families (Sellick, Thoburn and Philpot 2004).

Because of the issues discussed above, the study described in this book focuses on the close relationship between instability and delay and its effects on the very young children involved. It also explores how far the dominant view that children are best brought up by their birth families influenced decision-making in cases where parents were unable to safeguard their well-being, and identifies the characteristics of those parents who were able to overcome previous difficulties and eventually be reunited with their children.

Babies' needs

The emphasis in legislation and policy on promoting children's upbringing by their birth families wherever possible is informed not only by considerations of social justice, but also by a large body of research that demonstrates the importance of the development of attachment, particularly in the early years, as a basis for acquiring the ability to form secure and lasting relationships (see Bowlby 1979; Zeanah and Emde 1994). Most children form attachments to birth parents; even when parents' inability to meet their needs requires long-term separation, they nevertheless generally benefit from continuing contact. The termination of the relationship with the birth family can create an enduring sense of loss and potentially damage the child's sense of self-esteem and 'lovability' (Schofield 2001), as well as their educational and psychological development (Brodzinsky *et al.* 1984).

However the *quality* of children's relationships with their birth parents or other primary carers is also fundamentally important to their physical, psychological, emotional and behavioural development (Howe 2001). The wider study from which the 42 babies were identified (Skuse *et al.* 2001) had shown that a high proportion of these young children became looked after because they had either been abused by their carers or were at risk of significant harm. Chapter 2 discusses their circumstances and those of their parents in some detail. Abuse and neglect have been found to lead to insecure patterns of attachment (Ainsworth *et al.* 1978; Crittenden 1995; Howe *et al.* 1999; Main 1995). Howe, Shemmings and Feast (2001) identify how young children will adapt their behaviour to cope with and survive inconsistent, unresponsive and/or hostile caregiving. This strategy, while functional in an adverse environment, is not functional in other social contexts. Those who experience sensitive and psychologically available caregiving are able to explore, experiment and play, facilitating psychological understanding and competence. In contrast, children who experience abuse and neglect risk 'suffering developmental impairments, behaviour problems and relationship difficulties; in many cases there is evidence of discontinuity with children showing good psychosocial outcomes' (Howe 2001, p.224).

In those cases where separation is necessary, early separations, within the first six months of a child's life, are thought to be less damaging than later separations, as at this stage, infants' interest in caregivers is more indiscriminate, what Howe (2001) terms 'attachment-in-the-making'. In the very early stages, having positive interactions *per se* matters more than interacting with specific people (Tannenbaum and Forehand 1994). Between the ages of 6 and 18 months, however, the loss of a prime attachment figure can lead to considerable distress and 'multiple breaks can lead to the child being virtually unable to make true relationships' (Jones *et al.* 1991, p.118), while a child who has successfully formed a secure attachment is able to go on to form others.

Many of these babies therefore needed to experience sensitive and consistent caregiving, with opportunities to develop secure attachments. Much of this book focuses on the evidence of change and instability in the lives of these very young children because such experiences are likely to have an impact on their ability to form secure attachments and can be seen as potentially detrimental to their long-term well-being. Preliminary evidence that family circumstances may have prevented some of these children from developing secure attachments with birth parents and that, once they entered the care system, such opportunities may have been further denied them because of the frequent changes of placement that so many experienced, obviously needed further investigation. Chapter 3 looks in some detail at the experience of loss and change in these babies' lives, from birth onwards, both while living with families and while looked after; it explores the reasons for changes and the inter-relationship between changes of address, changes of carer and changes of household.

There were also concerns about the length of time children spent looked after before achieving permanence. As stability is so important to babies, anything that causes delay to their living in a permanent family situation is likely to have a negative impact on them. Quinton, Rutter and Gulliver (1990) found that lengthy periods in non-permanent placements had a cumulative adverse effect on child development, even when the quality of care was high. In contrast, early permanent placement is associated with a lower risk of future problems. Rutter and the ERA Study Team (1998) also undertook a study of Romanian children placed for adoption in Britain; those placed before reaching six months old showed substantial improvements in cognitive and physical development. Although those placed when they were older also showed improved development, a higher proportion of the latter group showed evidence of peer relation problems and aberrant behaviour, difficulties thought to relate to longer exposure to severe deprivation.

Lowe and Murch (2002) have found that duration of time spent in care and movement are indicators of a high risk of adoptive placement breakdown. Further research evidence demonstrates that placement breakdown is more likely for older children (Berridge 1999; Maluccio, Pine and Warsh 1996; Triseliotis 2002); however some of the placements of babies in our study also disrupted, an issue which we explore in Chapter 3. Placement with siblings is thought to reduce the risk of breakdown (Thoburn 2002) but, as we discuss in Chapter 4, this was one of the reasons for delay in achieving permanence for the babies in our study.

What do we know about babies in care?

Surprisingly little is known about the experiences of very young children in care and accommodation. Much of the research into children's experiences has focused on older children, with a wealth of literature on young adults' experiences post care (Biehal *et al.* 1995; Courtney, Terao and Bost 2004; Dixon and Stein 2002; Kufeldt and Stein 2005). However there has been virtually no research that has focused on the needs and experiences of babies and very young children placed away from home. Until the 1970s, large numbers of very young children in Britain were voluntarily placed for adoption, and spent a brief period with foster carers before being permanently placed with adoptive parents. Since then, the virtual disappearance of the stigma previously attached to single parenthood, as well as the availability of contraception and the legalisation of abortion have meant that very few babies are voluntarily relinquished. Comparison with the United States would suggest that the Adoption Act 1976, which removed the provision for third party adoptions and strengthened the position of local authorities, may also have influenced the situation in Britain (see Schulman and Behrman 1993). Virtually all children in Britain who are eventually placed for adoption outside their extended families have now previously spent a lengthy period in care or accommodation; they are likely to have had difficult and damaging experiences prior to becoming looked after, although freeing orders are often contested (see Chapter 4).

> Adoption of children from care in the 21st century is less about providing homes for relinquished babies and more concerned with providing

secure, permanent relationships for some of society's most vulnerable children. (Department of Health 2000a, p.5)

Although there has been an acknowledgement that changes need to be made to the process of adoption to meet the changing needs of children awaiting adoptive placements (Department of Health 2000b), without evidence such as that provided by the experiences of the children described in this book, it is difficult to move away from the assumption that babies who enter care and who cannot quickly return home are likely to follow the relatively straightforward and swift pathways to adoption that previous generations experienced. However it is gradually becoming evident that worryingly high numbers of very young children experience lengthy delays and multiple changes of placement while looked after (Ivaldi 2000). One of the very few pieces of research that focuses specifically on babies is that by Cousins and colleagues (2003), who examined care careers and placement stability of children aged under five years in Northern Ireland in a study population of 407 in 11 Health and Social Services Trusts. Over the two-year period of their study, 48 per cent of the children experienced no changes of main carer; but 13 per cent experienced three or more, including one child who had seven placements (Cousins *et al.* 2003, pp.39–40). This study also found that, as children's ages increased, their chances of achieving permanency decreased. Ivaldi's survey of adoptions in 1998–1999 also revealed that, prior to placement for adoption, 44 per cent of infants between 1 and 12 months old had four or more changes of placement (Ivaldi 2000, p.111). The 42 babies in our study were, like those in both these other studies, all very young at admission to care or accommodation but, as Chapter 4 demonstrates, there were concerns that the long delays before permanence was achieved may have been similarly detrimental to their long-term well-being.

Changes to policy and practice during the course of the study

The 42 babies were all under one year old when they entered care or accommodation, between 1 April 1996 and 31 March 1997. We traced their life pathways from birth until 1 April 2002, by which time they were aged five or six. During that period there were numerous policy initiatives, intended to address some of the problems inherent in the care system identified above. It is important to be aware of these initiatives because they provide a background to the experiences of the children we were studying; moreover, as the research was conducted retrospectively, professionals who had been involved with the babies and their families were aware of such changes and were able to comment on their impact on services. We briefly introduce the key policy changes here, while our concluding chapter asks whether their impact is likely to have improved the situation of very young children who have since entered care or accommodation in England and Wales.

During the time that the children were looked after a major policy initiative was introduced, with the aim of transforming the management and delivery of social services for children in England. 'Quality Protects' was part of the wider government agenda on reducing social exclusion and modernising social services (Department of Health 1998b). The five-year programme ran from 1999 to 2004, and focused on improving services and, by implication, the outcomes achieved by all children in need, including children in child protection systems, children looked after by local authorities, disabled children and others receiving support from social services. The programme was linked to the development of government objectives for children's services and accompanying performance targets (Department of Health 1999a, 1999b, 2001a).

Within the Quality Protects framework, specific initiatives were introduced to address some of the issues of particular concern in the experiences of our 42 babies and other looked after children. Three of the original six priority areas focused on placement choice; assessment, care planning and recording; and improving life chances of looked after children. Plans to improve service delivery in these areas formed the focus of local authority management action plans, and progress was reviewed annually (Robbins 1999, 2000, 2001). The 'Choice Protects' initiative, launched in 2002, is a continuation of Quality Protects, and aims to support local authorities to improve outcomes by providing better placement stability, matching and choice.

The *Framework for the Assessment of Children in Need and their Families* (Department of Health, Department for Education and Employment and

Home Office 2000) was launched as part of the Quality Protects agenda and implemented in 2000, after these children had entered care or accommodation. Its purpose was to improve outcomes for children in need by ensuring that 'referral and assessment processes discriminate effectively between different types and levels of need and produce a timely service response' (Department of Health, Department for Education and Employment and Home Office 2000, p.xi). The *Framework* reflects a holistic approach to work with children and families and requires practitioners to assess the inter-relationship between children's developmental needs and the capacities of parents and carers to respond to them within the wider family and environmental context.

On a more local level, the introduction of concurrent planning is intended to reduce delays in decision-making where it seems probable that children will not be able to return home. This initiative was developed in the United States to promote timely decision-making and aimed 'to speed up the placement of children into permanent families, specifically to prevent drift and delay' (Monck, Reynolds and Wigfall 2003, p.5). Concurrent planning aims to place children with foster carers who are able to work with parents to promote rehabilitation, but who will later adopt the child, if reunification proves not to be possible. The role of concurrent planning in permanently placing very young children was being evaluated during the course of our study (Monck *et al.* 2003).

The Adoption Act 1976 was still in force at the time the research was undertaken, although preparations were underway to reform adoption law, following recognition of shifts in adoption trends. The White Paper on *Adoption* (Department of Health 2000b) outlined the government's intention to promote the wider use of adoption as a permanent solution for children who are unable to remain with or return to, their families, to minimise delay in the adoption process and to establish a register of children waiting to be adopted and approved adoptive families. The Adoption and Children Bill was before parliament during 2001, at the time social work practitioners were being interviewed as part of this study. As practitioners were familiar with these developments, it was possible to explore in what ways they expected the proposed legislation to influence decision-making for babies looked after by local authorities in the future (see Chapter 5).

The Adoption and Children Act was enacted in 2002 and aligns adoption legislation with the Children Act 1989. In both Acts the child's welfare must be the paramount consideration (Adoption and Children Act 2002 Section 1(1); Children Act 1989 Section 1(1)).

The law, policy and practice are not static, but continually evolving. Since the completion of the study further developments have taken place, many in response to the tragic death of Victoria Climbié in 2002 (Laming 2003). The new policy initiative, *Every Child Matters* (HM Government 2003), is supported by the Children Act 2004 and emphasises how all agencies with responsibilities for children need to work together in order to help all children achieve the five key outcomes that they themselves have identified as being important to them: be healthy, stay safe, enjoy and achieve, make a positive contribution and achieve economic well-being (p.4). These outcomes have been described as universal ambitions for all children and young people, irrespective of their background or circumstances (Department for Education and Skills 2004a). The emphasis on outcomes is of particular relevance to the experiences of the very young children we studied.

Chapter 5 considers how far changes introduced by the new policy agenda, as well as by new legislation on adoption and the Modernising Social Services programme, are likely to influence decision-making for very young looked after children in the future. It will, of course, be some time before real evidence of change emerges from the more recent initiatives. Messages for practice identified throughout this book need to be considered with reference to these numerous policy developments.

The 42 babies

The 42 babies who form the focus of this book were originally identified because they were part of a larger group of 242 children looked after by six local authorities, all of whom entered care or accommodation within the same timeframe and were looked after for at least a year (see Skuse *et al.* 2001; Skuse and Ward 2003; Ward and Skuse 1999; Ward *et al.* forthcoming a). One of the early findings from this wider study was that very young children, admitted to care or accommodation before their first birthday, were substantially over-represented in this group who remained long looked after, accounting for 17 per cent (42) of the total. This wider study had also shown that the initial plans for these babies had almost all been for a time-limited assessment or an early return to their birth family, and that only four had become looked after with a care plan that envisaged adoption or long-term placement with foster carers. It had also found that, while they were looked after, these very young children had experienced several changes of placement, some of which had disrupted (Skuse *et al.* 2001). As must be obvious from the preceding discussion, it was important to ask some detailed questions about the experiences of these very vulnerable young children because this evidence from the wider study raised significant issues relating to the extent to which legislation, policy and practice were – or were not – supporting and delivering a service that met their needs.

Methodology

The larger group consisted of *all* the children who had been placed in the care of the participating authorities between 1 April 1996 and 31 March 1997, and were still looked after on 1 April 1998. They came from six English local authorities, deliberately chosen to reflect both geographical and organisational diversity. The authorities included an inner and an outer London borough, two shire counties, a metropolitan district and a new unitary. They were selected on the grounds that they would be nationally representative of all local authorities; the characteristics of the group of children identified should therefore reflect those of the population of children who entered long-term care in England towards the end of the 1990s (Ward and Skuse 1999, p.7).

Extensive quantitative data had been collected from case files on each of the 242 children in the wider study, relating to their needs, the services they received and their developmental progress, at entry to the care system, at 1 April 1998, 30 September 1999 and 30 September 2000. These were the data that had demonstrated that the preponderance of very young children in the wider study, and their experiences of change and delay would merit further exploration. However, a more detailed approach, which encompassed both quantitative and qualitative research methods, was considered necessary to examine further the reasons for the experiences of these 42 babies.

A number of studies (see for example Millham *et al.* 1986; Minty 1999; Packman and Hall 1998; Sinclair and Gibbs 1998; Sinclair, Wilson and Gibbs 2000) have focused on children's experiences while looked after. However, children's experiences prior to entry to care are also likely to influence their long-term development and outcomes, and the ages of these children meant that it was possible to note all significant events and changes experienced from birth onwards. A comprehensive case-file search was therefore conducted to trace chronologically all the changes experienced by each of the 42 babies from when they were born until they ceased to be looked after (or 1 April 2002, if still in care or accommodation).[1] Chronological information included all changes of primary carer, household composition and address. An address was defined as anywhere a child stayed for one or more nights and therefore could include hospital, the child's birth home, any subsequent homes he or she lived in, any foster homes or other placements.[2] If a child returned to a previous address this was counted again. Because the children were so young we decided that *any* change of address might be regarded as important, and so we recorded all moves that could be identified, even if they were only for one or two nights. Changes of care plan and legal status were also included in the chronology. All these events were then mapped alongside the reasons for change, including action taken by courts, social services, parents and carers. Given the detrimental impact of delay on welfare outcomes for children, the duration of delays in decision-making and actions and their causes were also noted.

Case-file data were supplemented by semi-structured interviews held with social workers, team leaders, family placement workers and children's guardians. Table 1.1 gives further details of the interviews conducted.[3] Attempts were made to interview all those who had held case management responsibilities for each child. Where children had had several social workers, or a number of team leaders had been involved, interviews were restricted to two practitioners: the one who had first become involved and the one who had most recently held the case. Interviews with social workers and team leaders related to their recollections of the specific case(s) and wider resource and policy issues that may have influenced the decision-making process and the children's life pathways. The majority of cases were closed by the time interviews were held; synopses based on the case-file data were therefore provided to aid recall.

Table 1.1 Interviews conducted

Interviewees	Number of interviews
Social workers	38
Team leaders	21
Family placement workers	11
Children's guardians	22
Assistant directors	6
Local authority solicitors	6
Chief clerks (family proceedings)	6
Current carers	8
Birth parents	4
Total	122

In each local authority semi-structured interviews were also held with the local authority solicitor, the chief clerk of the family proceedings court and the assistant director of children and families services; these covered wider organisational resource and policy issues, implementation of new initiatives, and participants' views of the potential implications of legislative changes introduced subsequent to the completion of the study.

In addition to the professionals, birth parents and current carers were also approached for interview if they had been involved in the decision-making process and if the local authorities considered it appropriate to contact them and had a current address. The research team received contact details for 11 birth mothers and six birth fathers. A number of addresses were found to be incorrect, and some birth parents were not at home at the times arranged to visit (see Clapton 2003; Munro, Holmes and Ward 2005). In the event, four birth parents were interviewed. These interviews focused on the extent to which birth parents felt involved in decisions, how and why they thought certain actions had been taken by social services and what they would have liked the outcome of the case to be. Where the child had returned home, parents were also asked about the reunification process and how they felt their child was doing now.

Eight current foster and adoptive carers agreed to be interviewed. Some current carers had already participated in two rounds of interviews as part of the wider study, which had followed up children and young people who had left care or accommodation during the study period (Skuse and Ward 2003); some adoptive parents had not anticipated further contact with social services and declined the invitation to participate. Others had previously declined to be interviewed and therefore were not re-contacted. A combination of these factors is likely to explain their low response rate.

Those current carers, including birth parents, who were interviewed also completed the Strengths and Difficulties Questionnaire – a validated instrument intended to indicate the type and significance of emotional and behavioural difficulties displayed by individual children (Goodman 1997; Goodman, Meltzer and Bailey 1998).

Interview data were analysed thematically both by case and also by professional group. This approach was intended both to identify different perspectives at case level and also to make it easier to explore any divergence in policy interpretation and implementation at different levels within and between social services and the court arena.

Limitations of the research

It should be acknowledged that the study had a number of limitations that affect the reliability and generalisability of the findings. First, the number of children (42) was small, thus affecting the strength of the evidence overall, and particularly that relating to sub-groups of children within the sample studied, such as those who were part of a sibling group or who were permanently placed with fathers. A low response rate from carers also limited the value of data on long-term outcome.

Second, although a small number of babies who had spent well over a year in care or accommodation were found in each of the six participating local authorities, they formed over 20 per cent of the children from two of these. Over half the babies (55%; 23 out of the 42) came from the metropolitan district, Authority E. This local authority was the largest and therefore contributed the greatest number of children to the wider study; nevertheless, a substantially disproportionate percentage of these (27%) were babies. In contrast, one of the shire counties, Authority F, contributed the second largest number, 60 children, to the full group, but only included seven (11%) babies. The reasons for these disparities are explored further in Chapter 2. However, the fact that they were so extensive suggests that the sample may be somewhat skewed towards children with the type of needs and experiences shown by those from this metropolitan district.

Furthermore, it should be emphasised that this research focuses on very young children who spent lengthy periods in care or accommodation. We did not have the necessary data to compare their experiences with those of other young children who were more quickly reunited with their families or who remained at home with support from a range of children's and adults' services, although a subsequent study (Ward, Munro and Caulfied forthcoming b) is now aiming to fill this gap.

The intensive study of the life pathways of these 42 babies has focused on three key questions. First, we sought to understand the quality of the children's experiences by tracing life histories and exploring the frequency and reasons for changes of address, carer and household members, both prior to entry to care or accommodation and while the babies were looked after. Second, we identified the causes of delay in the decision-making process, and analysed the relationship between drift and instability; third, we focused on final outcomes, viewed in the context of these young children's life pathways, both within and outside the care system.

Introducing the babies

There is always a danger that in presenting research, the individual children are forgotten. While the book explores key themes and issues that affected the life pathways of the group as a whole, each of the babies we studied had his or her own unique history and different experiences both prior to entry to care and while being looked after. We end this chapter by introducing the reader to some of the children to whom we later refer most frequently. In order to preserve confidentiality some minor details have been changed in all the case studies referred to in this book; however none of these details relate to the issues that the children's experiences are used to illustrate.

May

May is a girl of white British origin. Her elder brother had been physically abused by their father, and May was placed on the child protection register prior to birth because she too was considered to be at risk of neglect and physical abuse. However, by the time she was born the relationship between her parents had ended. May and her mother both entered a residential unit where an assessment of her mother's parenting capacity could be undertaken. Before the assessment was complete, May's mother left the unit, taking the child with her, but returned for a few days following discussions with social services. After this happened a second time, May was placed with foster carers. Her mother's attendance at contact was sporadic and concerns were also raised that she had resumed her relationship with May's father. May was placed with adoptive carers ate the age of 13 months.

Kathryn

Kathryn is a girl of white British origin, who suffered a serious non-accidental head injury when she was less than a month old and developed complex health needs as a result. On discharge from hospital she was placed with foster carers. Following assessment, a plan for adoption was agreed when Kathryn was six months old. The foster parents considered applying to adopt her, but then decided they would prefer to foster her on a long-term basis. At the end of the study, Kathryn was still looked after and living with her original foster carers.

Natasha

Natasha is a girl of white British origin. After she was born, her mother developed post-natal depression and her father took on the role of primary carer. When she was two months old, Natasha was taken to hospital with a fractured femur, suspected to be a non-accidental injury. She was accommodated under the Children Act 1989 (Section 20), and later a care order was granted. A comprehensive assessment was undertaken and Natasha returned home to both parents, aged eight months. A year and a half later the care order was discharged.

Matt

Matt is a boy of mixed white and African Caribbean origin with two older sisters, both of whom had been placed on the child protection register under the category of neglect before he was born. Matt's mother took drugs during the pregnancy and at birth he experienced drug withdrawal symptoms. Following discharge from hospital Matt lived with his mother and sisters and had regular contact with his grandparents. When his father was released from prison and returned to the family home, Matt's mother moved into a homeless hostel with the three children. When Matt had an asthma attack his mother took him to hospital, but the doctor noted that she was under the influence of drugs and referred the case to social services. Given social services' concern about their mother's chaotic lifestyle and drug taking, an Emergency Protection Order was granted and Matt and his sisters were placed together in foster care. He was then seven months old. An assessment was undertaken and a plan for adoption agreed. The children had three changes of foster carers and on one occasion Matt was separated from his sisters. Attempts were made to find an ethnically matched adoptive placement for the sibling group, but these proved unsuccessful. At the age of three years seven months, Matt was finally placed with adoptive carers, while his sisters remained with the last set of foster carers on a long-term basis.

Beth

Beth is a girl of white British origin. Her mother took drugs during the pregnancy and at birth Beth experienced drug withdrawal symptoms. Following discharge from hospital Beth lived with her mother. Both the health visitor and family centre provided support and monitored Beth's care. After a month, a number of anonymous referrals were received by social services concerning Beth's care, although when home visits were made she appeared well. When Beth was ten months old, her mother requested accommodation for her daughter as she felt unable to cope, but she then refused the placements offered. Beth then spent time living with a number of relatives before being accommodated by the local authority under the Children Act 1989 (Section 20) aged 11 months. An interim care order was granted four months later due to increasing concerns about Beth's mother's lifestyle and drug use. A place was secured for Beth's mother in a drug rehabilitation unit, with a view to Beth joining her later; however, shortly before this was due to happen, the mother left the unit and disappeared. The decision to plan for adoption was taken when Beth was aged one year eight months. The first freeing application was refused, but granted on appeal, and Beth was placed with adoptive carers when she was just over two years old.

Harry

Harry is a boy of white British origin, who was born with foetal alcohol syndrome and had complex health needs. Before his birth his elder sister had been placed in the care of the local authority because of his father's violence and both parents' misuse of alcohol. His mother was also ambivalent about his birth. Harry was registered as at risk of physical harm at a pre-birth child protection conference. A police protection order was granted the day Harry was born, because his mother threatened to remove him from hospital against advice. Shortly afterwards an interim care order was granted. A residential assessment of parenting capacity was initiated, but broke down due to violence between Harry's parents. Harry was placed with foster carers before he was one month old, and shortly afterwards a plan for adoption was agreed. Harry's foster carers wished to be considered as adoptive parents but the local authority did not support their application because of their age. Harry subsequently moved to alternative foster carers before being placed with prospective adoptive carers when he was one year and three months old.

Conclusion

The following chapters of this book use information such as that shown in the above case studies to offer an in-depth exploration of the life pathways of all 42 very young children both before, during and after the time that they were looked after by local authorities (Chapter 2). They attempt to disentangle the complex relationship between instability and delay and to identify findings that would be of value for the development of practice and policy in this area (Chapters 3 and 4). In Chapters 2, 3 and 4, specific points for practice are signalled as concluding notes. Throughout the book, the babies' experiences need to be understood within a context in which policy in this area is continually changing to try to modernise and improve the care system. The concluding chapter draws together the practice issues, and explores the implications of our findings for policy. It discusses how far changes that have since been made would address some of the difficulties encountered by the children we studied.

Notes

1 Data were collected from 41 case files. In one case, where the case file was not available, data from the longitudinal study and management information data were utilised.

2 Regular secondary placements in a particular household were only counted once.

3 Throughout this book, those tables which present information the reader may need to have readily available are included in the text, while others, which provide supplementary information, are placed in the Appendix.

Chapter 2

Forty-two Babies

Their Circumstances, Characteristics and Life Pathways

Introduction

This chapter focuses on the experiences of the 42 babies who spent a lengthy period in care or accommodation before achieving permanence. It traces their life pathways in order to shed further light on their circumstances, characteristics and experiences before, during and after the time that they were looked after. It explores why disproportionate numbers of children came from two authorities. It also considers the information we have on the children's circumstances at the end of the study (five years after admission) and seeks to understand how their experiences are likely to have affected their long-term development and well-being.

The 42 babies had all been placed in the care of a local authority before their first birthday, and had remained there for at least a year. The fact that they were looked after at such an early age and for so long suggests that these very young children had been born into vulnerable birth families living in very difficult situations and contending with numerous problems. The babies whose life histories we were able to explore may well have had very different experiences and outcomes from other young children who were born into similar situations but either had much shorter periods in care or accommodation or remained with their birth families throughout their childhood, perhaps with help from family support services. A subsequent study, currently being undertaken by the research team is seeking to explore this question further (Ward *et al.* forthcoming b).

The babies' characteristics

The babies were a sub-group, taken from a much wider group of children who stayed long in care in the six participating authorities, and were studied by the research team for several years (Skuse *et al.* 2001; Skuse and Ward 2003; Ward and Skuse 2001; Ward *et al.* forthcoming a). Many characteristics such as dual or multiple heritage, health conditions, or parental substance abuse were evident in the larger group of children and have been shown to be indicators of their own vulnerability and the fragility of their families; such characteristics were also present among the babies, but perhaps because of their extreme youth, are more evidently risk factors that can reduce children's chances of successful outcomes.

Of the 42 babies, half were boys and half girls. Most (29) were of white British origin, although ten were of mixed heritage, with the greatest number of the latter group being White Asian (4) and White–Black Caribbean (4). One child was Black Caribbean and two were Irish.

While over half (27) of these very young children appeared to be healthy, 15 were reported to have health problems (see Appendix, Table A.1 for further details). Four babies had asthma and one, eczema. One had cerebral palsy and another a hearing impairment. In eight other cases, health conditions were attributable to the care the children had received prior to becoming looked after. Four babies whose mothers were drug users suffered from withdrawal symptoms at birth, now known to indicate a high risk of persistent and long-standing developmental difficulties (Moe 2002; Moe and Slinning 2003; Slinning 2003). Two others had foetal alcohol syndrome, and two had sustained non-accidental head injuries and had complex needs as a result. Both head injuries and foetal alcohol syndrome may damage the central nervous system and result in a range of abnormalities and behavioural problems (Abel 1997; Cleaver, Unell and Aldgate 1999). Health problems meant that many of these children were difficult to care for in infancy; as we shall see, their health at birth also continued to affect their future care and life experiences.

Family circumstances

As one might expect, information from the case-papers and interviews revealed that many of these very young children came from extremely vulnerable families who had difficulty in meeting what were often complex needs. Bebbington and Miles (1989) found that living with a lone parent was the most powerful of a range of factors that precipitate children into the care system. At entry to care or accommodation, 28 of the 42 babies were living with a single parent (27 with their mothers and one with a father); however 12 were living with both parents, and two with their mothers and their partners – or would have been, had they not become looked after from birth.

Within the families, nine of the children had no siblings, nine had full siblings, 16 had half siblings and another eight had a mixture of full and half siblings. Two children also had siblings who had died. Family sizes ranged from one to nine children; 28 of these babies had at least one sibling who was also looked after. As will become apparent, the complexity of family relations and the desire to find families to meet the cultural needs of sibling groups of different mixed heritage had important implications for the matching process.

Many of the babies came from families where the parents had substantial problems. Three of the mothers and four of the fathers were misusing alcohol, seven mothers and two fathers were misusing drugs, and one mother and one father were misusing both. In addition, a total of five mothers were homeless and two of these were also drug users. There was also a high incidence of reported domestic violence, involving 11 families. Eight of the mothers lacked family support and four mothers were reported as having a 'chaotic lifestyle'. Given these particular family circumstances – the high incidence of alcohol- and drug-related problems, violence, homelessness and lack of family support, it is perhaps not surprising that eight of the mothers were suffering from depression or had other mental health problems. Table 2.1 shows the extent of mothers' difficulties indicating that more than half (24/41) of them had some problems with drugs, alcohol, mental ill health, domestic violence or a combination of these. Cleaver and colleagues (1999) suggest that:

> While caution is needed in making assumptions about the impact on children of parental mental illness, problem alcohol or drug use or domestic violence, if the issues coexist the risk to the children increases considerably. (p.23)

(for further discussion see Kroll and Taylor 2003). In total, eight babies had mothers with multiple conditions. Cousins and colleagues (2003, p.64) found that the presence of multiple conditions such as these was associated with higher levels of instability in children's care careers.

Table 2.1: Mothers' problems

	Number of mothers[a] (n=41)	Percentage
No problems	17	41
Drug problem	5	12
Alcohol problem	1	2
Mental ill health	5	12
Domestic violence	5	12
Drug and alcohol problem	1	2
Drug and mental ill health	1	2
Drug and domestic violence	2	5
Alcohol and domestic violence	2	5
Mental ill health and domestic violence	2	5
Total	41	98[b]

a There was one set of twins in the sample, and therefore 41 mothers.

b Percentages do not add up to 100 due to rounding.

Although 17 of the babies had mothers who had no problems in relation to alcohol or drug use, mental health or domestic violence, this is not to suggest that they were problem free. Two of these mothers had mild learning disabilities and two were very young and immature (one being a minor and herself in the care of the local authority). Five of these mothers had financial problems, and one had been dealing, but not apparently using drugs, and was in prison when social services became involved with the family. The majority of these 17 mothers were found to have poor parenting skills and their babies were either neglected or subjected to non-accidental injury.

Drawing on Cleaver and Freeman's (1995) typology of the families of children in need, it is apparent that these babies came from families with multiple problems, greatly increasing the potential risks to them and the likelihood that they would suffer significant harm. It would have been useful to explore the relationship between parenting problems noted above and other issues such as parental offending behaviour, unemployment, benefit receipt and housing. However such information was too infrequently recorded in case files to allow for any meaningful analysis (see also Ward *et al.* forthcoming a).

Local authorities

The information about the children's characteristics and family circumstances sheds some light on the question of why some local authorities had a higher proportion of babies than others in their long-stay population of looked after children. As we indicated in Chapter 1, this book on the babies' experiences while looked after came about as a direct result of a larger study of long looked after children in six local authorities (Ward *et al.* forthcoming a). It is only by looking at this wider study that we can examine differences between the local authorities, as the total number of children in the earlier study was significantly larger, at 242, than this smaller subset of the 42 babies, all of whom were drawn from within that original group.

In the wider group of looked after children of all ages studied by the research team (Ward *et al.* forthcoming a), more than a fifth of those from Authorities D (a unitary authority) and E (a metropolitan authority) were babies who had started to be looked after before their first birthdays. This was particularly noteworthy in Authority E, where 23 (27%) from a total of

86 children fell within this age group. Subsequent interviews with professionals within the local authorities gave no indication that the court processes were any more efficient or that social work decision-making was better focused in the other authorities. However, there was evidence that the types of need and family circumstances that have been identified as characteristic of these very young children who stay long in care were more prevalent in these authorities, particularly in the large metropolitan Authority E.

Further, in the wider group of looked after children studied, those from Authority E were much more likely to have had parents who were neglectful or had a chaotic lifestyle than were those from the other authorities. Such behaviour patterns are often related to drug addiction, particularly high among parents of the children from this authority. They may also be related to alcohol misuse or poor mental health, although the incidence of these problems was no more striking in this authority than in others. However, this authority did have by far the lowest proportion of long looked after children whose parents did *not* appear to be neglectful, to have mental health problems, to misuse drugs or alcohol, or to have a chaotic lifestyle. As we shall see, these parental problems tended to prevent children from returning home; for younger children in particular, rehabilitation would have been unsafe until they could be addressed. As later chapters of this book will demonstrate, when children could not swiftly return to parents, the process of finding robust permanent solutions was complex and accounted for protracted stays in care. This may go some way towards explaining the preponderance of very small children from this authority.

In the case of the metropolitan Authority E, this evidence is further supported by the fact that for 80 per cent of children long looked after, the primary reason for entry to care or accommodation was abuse, neglect, or parental illness, which in most cases was identified as drug or alcohol addiction or mental health problems. Once again, these are reasons why very small children in particular could not swiftly go home. The pattern was substantially different in the other authorities (see Appendix, Figure A.1).

A number of wider socio-economic factors may render families more vulnerable and lead to an increased demand for services (see Carr-Hill *et al.*

1997). Population density, as expected, was substantially higher than the national average in the two London authorities (A and B). Authority E also had a population density three times higher than the national average. This was also the only authority with a higher than national average number of lone parents. All of these indicators suggest that there would have been a higher demand for services in Authority E.

The picture in the unitary Authority D, however, was different. This authority only contributed 25 children to the wider study (Ward *et al.* forthcoming a), five (20%) of whom were babies. With such small numbers, the preponderance of babies might not be significant. However it is noteworthy that this authority also had a high percentage of children whose primary reason for admission was abuse or neglect. It also had a high percentage of children whose parents were neglectful, but none whose chaotic lifestyle, drug or alcohol abuse were seen as problematic, and only one whose parent(s) had mental health problems. This may be because adult services in this authority were better coordinated with children's services so that fewer children became looked after. Those that did, however, may have come from families with particularly intractable problems, so that they were unlikely to return home speedily.

The suggestion that the unitary Authority D may have been able to offer better support to families in the community and therefore prevent the need for any but the most disadvantaged children from becoming looked after is supported by evidence that those it did place away from home tended to be children with exceptional and complex needs who, perhaps, family support services were unlikely to be able to reach. For instance, when compared with the other authorities, D had a high proportion of long looked after children and young people in the wider study with a physical disability (11; 46%), or learning disability (12; 50%). These features are common to other authorities that have reduced their looked after population to a very small group, all of whom have complex needs and are likely to stay long in care (see Ward *et al.* 2004).

Social services involvement

Given the extent of vulnerability, it is not surprising that a very high proportion of the children (35) came from families that had had involvement with social services prior to their admission. Moreover case-files indicated that at least 17 mothers and 3 fathers had had some involvement with social services during their own childhoods and that 14 of these parents had themselves been looked after.

There is evidence that behaviour patterns may be repeated inter-generationally in early interactions between parents and children (Putallaz *et al.* 1998), suggesting that those who are abused or develop attachment problems may have parents whose childhood experiences were similar. Quinton and Rutter (1988, p.202) found that in almost all the families they studied with children taken into care, one or both parents reported marked adversities in their childhood, although inter-generational continuities looking forward were much weaker than continuities viewed retrospectively. Such evidence may shed some light on the high number of children whose parents had also had social services support during their own childhoods. Of particular importance here, however, is evidence that in at least two cases, social workers' previous relationships with mothers who had been looked after influenced the decisions that were made about their children.

Child protection registration

Parenting difficulties are further demonstrated by the very high proportion of the babies who had been placed on the child protection register prior to admission. Nineteen (45%) had been placed on the child protection register before they were born or at birth, most commonly because they were *at risk* of neglect or physical abuse. The perceived risk was commonly related to social services' previous involvement with the families in response to the neglect and/or physical abuse of siblings. A further 18 babies had been placed on the child protection register at a later date. The most common reason for registration at this stage was *actual* physical abuse. For nine of the babies the abuse included a combination of factors, mainly neglect and physical abuse; in two cases a risk of sexual abuse was also identified. In total only five of the 42 babies had not been placed on the child protection register (see Appendix, Table A.2 for further details).

Reasons for being placed in local authority care

Table 2.2 gives details of the primary reasons why the 42 babies were placed in care or accommodation.

Table 2.2: Primary reasons for the children's entry to care or accommodation (CIN categories)

	Number of children (n=42)	Percentage
Parental illness	9	21
Abuse/neglect	31	74
Family in acute stress	0	0
Family dysfunction	2	5
Total	42	100

Given that the majority of the babies had already been placed on the child protection register, it is not surprising that abuse or neglect was the primary reason for admission for over two thirds (31) of them. Case-files provided additional information. Ten of these babies were admitted because they were thought to be at risk after one of their siblings had sustained a non-accidental injury, although they themselves had *not* been abused. The definition of neglect used in England and Wales includes failing to protect a child from physical abuse or danger (Department of Health *et al.* 1999, p.15): in five of these cases it was acknowledged that the mother had not caused the injury but, rather, had failed to protect the child from significant harm. In a further seven cases babies had sustained non-accidental injuries. Two of these had been known to social services prior to hospital admission; in both these cases concerns had centred on their parents' age, maturity and ability to cope. In the majority of the remaining cases in which abuse or neglect was the primary factor, children were admitted in response to neglect or abandonment.

The second most frequent primary reason, accounting for nine of the babies' admissions, was parental illness or addiction. Drug, alcohol or mental health problems were the most prevalent parental conditions leading to their children's admission to care or accommodation. The remaining two of the babies became looked after because their families were considered to be dysfunctional: one had a mother who was in prison and a father who was unable to cope; the other had parents with long-standing social problems who were homeless at the time of the admission.

Changes of address and primary carers prior to admission

More than half (22) of the babies had started to be looked after before they were a month old, 12 were admitted between one and five months and 8 between six months and a year. These were, therefore, an extremely vulnerable group of very young children, most of whom had parents with problems that placed them at risk of significant harm. Consistency in primary carer and predictable routine, particularly for young infants, are recognised as instrumental in the development of secure attachments (Bowlby 1979; Bremner 1991; Lamb 1981). The parents of many of these children were struggling with problems that meant they were unable to offer this kind of stability. Therefore their children's experiences prior to entry to care or accommodation are likely to have influenced their sense of security, their ability to form attachments and, potentially, their long-term well-being.

We were interested to know whether the babies had changed address *prior* to their entry to care. This was considered to be an important factor, as frequent changes of address are indicative of instability. Because the children were so young, we decided any change of address should be noted; these included temporary moves from parents to other relatives or friends and also moves in and out of hospital for those babies with health problems. We included any change of address where the child stayed for one or more nights.

As Table 2.3 shows, almost one in four (9) of the babies had been placed in care or accommodation from birth. A further 12 had only one address prior to entry, meaning that exactly half (21; 50%) had no experience of instability before entry to care or accommodation. However, 7 had two or three and 11 had four or more addresses prior to becoming looked after; of these 18 children, 10 had parents who were misusing drugs or alcohol, or were suffering from mental ill health. Such problems also tended to exacerbate the financial and relationship difficulties that accounted for the frequent moves of many other parents.

Table 2.3: Number of addresses prior to being looked after

Number of addresses	Number of children (n=39)	Percentage
None (placed at birth)	9	23
One	12	31
Two or three	7	18
Four or more	11	28
Total	39	100

As well as changes of address, some babies also experienced changes in primary carer. Obviously the nine babies placed at birth had no previous carer. A further 12 had only one primary carer before becoming looked after; these are the same babies who had only lived at one address. However, nearly half the babies (18) had at least two primary carers before they became looked after, and five had four or more (see Table 2.4). These multiple changes of address and carer are likely to have impeded the attachment process. Furthermore, those babies who spent time in hospital may have experienced more inconsistency than we might expect, for it has been found that 'newborns in special care units settle down into a steady routine more rapidly if cared for by only a few nurses' (Bremner 1991, p.190), and we do not know how far this was their experience.

Table 2.4: Number of primary carers prior to entry

Number of primary carers	Count (n=39)	Percentage
None (placed at birth)	9	23
One	12	31
Two or three	13	33
Four or more	5	13
Total	39	100

Although some changes were attributable to hospital admissions, it was also evident that a number of the babies experienced changes of address and/or carer as a result of their parents' lifestyles or circumstances. The following example was typical of six cases where mothers had alcohol, drug and/or mental health problems and their children experienced over four addresses prior to becoming looked after.

Beth's case

Beth was born in hospital and then lived with her mother. Four months later they moved to her grandfather's house. Following an argument, Beth and her mother moved out and her mother resumed the role of primary carer. Shortly afterwards, Beth moved to her aunt's home for four days. They then moved in with her grandmother, who cared for Beth as her mother was suffering from drug withdrawal. After one month, the grandmother decided to return to work and Beth became looked after. By then she was 11 months old and had had six addresses and five primary carers. After admission, Beth remained with the same foster carers for 14 months, until she was placed with prospective adoptive carers.

Experiences while looked after

While some children, such as Beth, experienced relative stability once they had become looked after, this was not always the case. Some babies experienced instability and change both before and during their care episode, although overall there was little relationship between the number of changes prior to and post admission.

Local authorities are required to record details of all placements of looked after children.[1] During the first year that they were looked after, 14 of the babies had one placement and 17 had three or more; 3 children in this latter group had five placements. The rate of movement had slowed down by the second year, but there was still quite a high level of instability: in the second 12 months half of the babies had one placement and six had three or more; one child in the latter group had four placements and another one six. Moreover changes of *placement* do not include brief periods of fewer than seven days that children spend in hospital or in temporary homes while carers are away. For very young children such temporary moves are likely to be distressing, particularly if they have little previous experience of continuity and stability. As with the period before children entered care or accommodation, throughout the care episode in this study we were able to track all changes of address, however brief. Table 2.5 shows that more than half the babies had four or more addresses during the time they were looked after (between 14 and 69 months). Of the thirteen children who had six or more addresses were one child who had nine, one who had eleven and one who had seventeen. Changes of address were not always accompanied by a change of primary carer. Nevertheless, as Table 2.6 shows, only four children retained the same primary carer throughout the time that they were looked after, and nineteen had four or more.

Table 2.5: *Number of addresses while looked after*

Number of addresses	Count (n=39)	Percentage
One	2	5
Two	7	18
Three	4	11
Four to five	13	33
Six or more	13	33
Total	39	100

Table 2.6: Number of primary carers while looked after

Number of primary carers	Count (n=38)	Percentage
One	4	11
Two	9	24
Three	6	16
Four to five	15	39
Six or more	4	10
Total	38	100

It is important to acknowledge that in some instances, for example when a child moves to a prospective adoptive placement, the change represents a move towards greater continuity and stability. However the instability experienced by some children while they were looked after is likely to have further compounded insecurity, mistrust and difficulties associated with the caregiving they received in their early months of life.

Overall, the babies had between two and twenty-one addresses *from birth* until they ceased to be looked after, by which time they were aged between fifteen months and six years. Seven had three or fewer addresses while nineteen had seven or more; seven of these had experienced ten or more addresses between birth and exit from care. One might have expected that the older children would have had more addresses, but the facts do not appear to support this: nine of those aged over three had had seven or more addresses, as had nine of those aged between eighteen months and two and a half years (see Appendix, Table A.3 for further details).

It is clear that a number of the babies experienced an undesirable level of unpredictability and instability, both before they entered care or accommodation and during the care episode. This may well have had adverse consequences for both their immediate and their long-term well-being. In Chapter 1 we reviewed the evidence concerning the development of attachments in very young children and discussed the potentially negative impact of frequent changes of caring arrangements. May's experiences, described below, indicate the impact changes can have on a child and the confusion that instability and constant change can bring. The adoptive carer also felt that this child's previous life experiences continued to influence her behaviour.

May's case

May had eight addresses from birth until she was placed with prospective adoptive carers when she was 13 months old. During this time she had six primary carers. Her adoptive mother said:

> When she first came for a fortnight she was very polite, 'yes',' no', did exactly as she was told…what I realised later was her foster mum had been on a few holidays and she'd taken her to another foster place for like a fortnight's respite, while she was away, so for a fortnight she was on her best behaviour and then after a fortnight when she realised she was staying her first word to me was 'No', and her first sentence was 'I don't want to'…I worry about her because she's got…the only way I can put it is a self destruct button…I'm sure it's a testing thing… How far can I push her before she won't love me anymore? (Adoptive mother)

'Permanent' homes

The babies' life pathways were followed from birth until 1 April 2002, by which time they were aged between five and six. As Table 2.7 demonstrates, by that stage all but three of them had ceased to be looked after. Over half (23) had been adopted. Fourteen had returned to birth parents, and two were permanently placed with other relatives. Two of the three children who were still looked after were placed with relatives pending a residence order. The third was permanently placed with local authority foster carers. What were the factors that made these routes to permanence more – or less – likely?

Table 2.7: Domiciles on 1 April 2002

	Count (n=42)	Percentage
Not looked after		
Adoptive parents	23	55
Birth mother	8	19
Birth father	4	9
Both birth parents	2	5
Other relative	2	5
Looked after		
Local authority foster carers	1	2
Relative foster carers	2	5
Total	42	100

Return to birth mothers

Eight of these young children returned to lone birth mothers, a further two returned to live with both their parents. Four of these were babies who had originally been admitted for time-limited assessment of their mothers' parenting capacity. In all these cases the babies had become looked after aged less than one month, because older siblings had sustained non-accidental injuries. In two cases it was acknowledged that the mothers had not caused the injury but, rather, had failed to protect older siblings from significant harm. These mothers had subsequently separated from and were no longer in contact with the partners who posed a risk to their children. In the other two cases professionals disputed whether or not the birth mother had caused the injury or failed to protect an older sibling from harm.

None of the babies returned to mothers who had problems with drugs or alcohol. Only one baby returned to a mother with mental health problems, and in this instance the father was also living in the home. None of the babies who had had more than three addresses before becoming looked after returned to their mothers.

Birth fathers

Four of the children returned to birth fathers under the protection of a residence order. One of these was a joint residence order, made between the father and the paternal grandmother. It should be emphasised that we cannot generalise about such experiences, as the numbers involved are so low. Nevertheless, the pathways of these children indicate an area that merits further consideration.

None of these babies had been living with their fathers at the time of admission. The babies' subsequent experiences emphasise the importance of undertaking careful assessments to ascertain a father's willingness and ability to care for a young child who has spent a long period in care or accommodation, particularly if he has previously been absent from the family home.

Decision-making in cases where children returned to fathers was largely reactive. In one case a relative placement broke down, and the father agreed to care for the child. Regular respite was later needed to support him in caring for his three children. In another case the child was placed permanently with the father following a residential assessment; however, poor health meant that he later returned the child to the mother's care. This was despite the mother's parenting capacity having been assessed and found to be insufficient, and despite a residence order having been granted in his favour. Emily's case, below, is that of another child, returned to her birth father who then proved unable to offer permanent care.

Emily's case

Emily lived with her mother and half-sister, Mary, from birth. Her mother struggled to cope and she suffered from depression so the children were both placed in a foster home until she felt able to resume care. Less than one month later they returned to their mother and weekend respite was provided. Emily then started spending weekends with her father and later, when she was aged two years ten months he became her sole carer. A residence order was subsequently granted in his favour. This arrangement broke down ten months later and Emily's grandparents became her primary carers.

> We said that we were fed up of her going from pillar to post and that she should come and have a stable life and come to us. (Grandmother)

Her grandmother felt that the frequent changes Emily had experienced had had an impact on her behaviour:

> She needs a lot of attention. And looking at her and [my own children] of the same age she does need far more attention. (Grandmother)

Information from the wider study of 242 children shows that it was common for children and young people of all ages to move between family members after they had left care or accommodation (Skuse and Ward 2003). Emily was one of several children who moved around their families until they found a relative who was able to make a long-term commitment to them. Her grandmother's comments demonstrate how such experiences of instability can have a long-term impact on children's well-being.

Friends and relatives

In addition to Emily, two other babies were placed with relatives when they ceased to be looked after, and two others had been permanently placed with relatives for over four years, despite the fact that they were still looked after by the local authority when the study ended, on 1 April 2002. Although placement with relatives was the least common permanent solution, it should be acknowledged that in a further six cases, relatives (5) and family friends (1) applied for residence orders; three later withdrew their applications, the other three were dismissed during court proceedings.

Anne's case

Anne was placed with her paternal grandparents at the age of three days, following her discharge from hospital. Although from an administrative perspective she remained looked after for nearly two years, she achieved physical and emotional permanence at this time and had continuity of address and carer throughout her early childhood. Furthermore, she also lived with her three older siblings, Luke, Dave and Kay. Regrettably the placement broke down for the eldest two siblings, Luke and Dave, both of whom had experienced long-standing emotional abuse while in their parents' care. Anne's grandparents facilitated regular contact to enable Anne and Kay to maintain their relationships with their brothers. Like Emily, Anne found a placement with grandparents who were committed to meeting her needs long term.

In other cases, however, it was evident that relatives had the desire to offer care and support, but were not necessarily able to sustain this. In four cases babies were left with relatives prior to entry to care. However, their age, work commitments or the child's needs meant they felt unable to provide a permanent home. In other cases relatives offered themselves as potential carers while the child was looked after; however these placements did not always offer a desirable level of stability, as is shown in Liz's case below.

Liz's case

At birth Liz was placed with her mother, on an interim care order. After seven months this placement was terminated, because of mounting concerns about her mother's drug use and lifestyle. An aunt and uncle offered to care for Liz, but the placement only lasted for a week because her aunt found that the presence of such a young child in the household was unsettling her own children. Liz was then placed in foster care for four months until her aunt and uncle offered to care for her again. The fostering panel approved this arrangement, although they had some reservations because the aunt and uncle were white British, whereas Liz was of mixed ethnicity. There had also been a previous incident of domestic violence. The stability of the placement was uncertain and at one point it was close to disruption. Liz also spent considerable time with her grandparents and after a year it was suggested she should live with them. An assessment was undertaken and found that Liz was happy in her placement and should not be moved. Shortly after April 2002 a residence order was granted in favour of Liz's aunt and uncle, by which time she was five and a half years old.

As one children's guardian pointed out, placement with relatives could be fraught with tensions:

> Families…they stick together, and it's not necessarily the safest place for children to be… You can get yourself into a terrible mess sometimes, if you place within the family, because I think it's much more difficult to retreat from that position. (Children's guardian)

Adoption

Twenty-three (55%) of the babies were ultimately adopted. We have already seen that a high proportion of the babies had mothers who had drug, alcohol or mental health problems and adoption was the most common permanent solution for these children as well as for those who came from families where domestic violence was an issue. A number of studies have shown that adoption can be unstable or unsatisfactory for some children (see Department of Health 1999c). However adoption does appear to offer a long-term permanent home and stability for these very young children. There was no evidence of adoptive placements breaking down for any of the babies in the study discussed in this book.

Predicting placement outcomes

The evidence appears to suggest that very young children who have been long looked after may eventually return to mothers who have previously been unable to provide adequate protection from abuse, but have since separated from a suspected perpetrator. We do not know how successful these reunifications are. Where these children return to other family members, however, there is evidence that long-term stability is not always achieved, particularly if they are placed with a father who was not previously living in their home. Very young children who have had frequent changes of address prior to long-term admission to care or accommodation are unlikely to return permanently to their birth parents: only one of the eleven babies in this study who had had four or more addresses prior to being looked after was eventually placed with a birth parent, and this was a father who had not previously lived with the child; all the others were adopted or found permanent homes with relatives. When children move from one family member to another, this might be interpreted as demonstrating the strength of kinship networks. However such experiences can be detrimental to very young children, who may become increasingly demanding and insecure if a stable home base cannot be quickly provided. Babies whose mothers have drug, alcohol or mental health problems, or who come from families where there is domestic violence, are unlikely to be able to return home if the difficulties cannot be quickly resolved; for these children adoption may prove a more viable long-term route to permanence.

The babies now: aged five to six years

It is important to acknowledge that many of the babies we studied were not easy to look after. Those who suffer drug withdrawal at birth, and those with foetal alcohol syndrome are likely to require higher levels of care to meet their needs; parents and others who have substantial problems themselves are unlikely to be able to meet these demands. This may be one of the reasons why some permanent placements with parents and relatives were so fragile.

Moreover it is clear that throughout their lives many of the babies experienced change, loss and instability. Although almost all had ceased to be looked after by 1 April 2002, some children's previous experiences may have had a long-term impact on their emotional and behavioural development. This issue was further explored in the interviews with current carers.

Eight foster or adoptive carers and one birth parent gave information about their children's development at the time of interview. This low response rate means that the information on long-term well-being is limited. The numbers are too small to allow for reliable comparisons between those who returned home and those who were adopted.

By the time of the interviews the 'babies' were aged between five and six years. Some of them were still having difficulty in achieving a sense of stability. For instance, Harry had foetal alcohol syndrome as a result of his mother's alcohol use during pregnancy. Although this continued to affect his health and well-being, his adoptive mother also thought that he was still not entirely secure, four and a half years after placement:

> All the problems and difficulties he's got are related to his foetal alcohol syndrome. He has a poor sleep pattern...he will wake several times...three and five times every night...he's got his own bedroom, but he's also got a bed in our room, and he's mostly in that bed...he still needs...to be able to put his hand out and know we are there. (Adoptive parent)

Another child, May, was physically healthy. Her adoptive mother felt that she might have low self-esteem, as a result of her experiences while looked after. She described how, occasionally she would destroy items, but could not explain why:

> She's such a love in every other way, she's kind, she's a really nice kid but she's just got this button and I'm frightened that you know if she is going to do something she regrets...and upset herself. May be...the longer she's here and she knows she's staying the better it might get. (Adoptive parent)

May's previous experiences have been described earlier in this chapter. At the time of interview she had been with her adoptive family for five years.

Six carers also completed the *Strengths and Difficulties Questionnaire*, designed to provide information on the significance of any emotional and behavioural difficulties the child might display (Goodman 1997). Carers of children with foetal alcohol syndrome or complex health needs also completed this assessment, but the results were excluded from the analysis as these children had many difficulties that were associated with their health needs.

The *Strengths and Difficulties Questionnaire* has five subscales: hyperactivity, emotional symptoms, conduct problems, peer problems and pro-social behaviour. All six children who were assessed fell within the normal band for overall development and two of them fell within the normal banding in *all* the five subscales. None of the children were showing peer problems or less than normal pro-social behaviour, but half (3) had a borderline or abnormal score on the conduct subscale and on the hyperactivity scale (see

Appendix, Table A.5 for further details). The number of children whose emotional and behavioural development was assessed is too small to draw any conclusions, but it should be noted that the problems some were beginning to demonstrate were also particularly prevalent for older looked after children who completed the *Strengths and Difficulties Questionnaire* in the full cohort (Skuse and Ward 2003, p.50). These are the type of difficulties that can eventually jeopardise placements or make children hard to place.

As we only looked at the emotional and behavioural development of a very small group of children at one point in time, we were not able to tell whether difficulties were improving or diminishing. However in their work on concurrent planning and permanent placements for young children, Monck and colleagues (2003) also used the *Strengths and Difficulties Questionnaire* to assess a similar group of children aged four and above at two time points; the first approximately six weeks after placement and the second 12 to 15 months later. They found that six weeks after placement emotional symptoms and pro-social behaviour scores were near the level expected of children of similar age who were living with their families. The proportion of borderline or abnormal scores was higher than that expected of children living with their families in relation to conduct problems, peer problems and hyperactivity. Twelve to fifteen months later, conduct problems were reported in fewer looked after children. Hyperactivity remained relatively high at both time points.

Conclusion

The children in our study were all extremely young when they entered care or accommodation. Over half of them came from families where birth parents were struggling with alcoholism, drug addiction or mental health problems. Almost all had experienced physical abuse or neglect before they became looked after, and many had moved frequently between homes and relatives before they were placed. They were looked after for between 14 and 69 months; 16 (40%) for 12 to 24 months, 11 (30%) for 25 to 36 months and 11 (30%) for 37 to 69 months. During that period some of them continued to experience constant loss and change. By April 2002, 23 had been adopted and 16 returned to birth parents or relatives, many of them with placements protected by a residence order. Some of the children who went home experienced further moves. It is not surprising that, five or six years after they had started to be looked after, some of the children were showing evidence of emotional and behavioural difficulties, and that carers were still trying to help them overcome the effects of early adverse experiences.

However, it should also be noted that not all the children were experiencing difficulties. Children looked after by local authorities are not a homogeneous group – they come with different needs and strengths and have varied experiences both during and after the care episode (see Skuse and Ward 2003). While many of these children experienced continuing loss and instability while they were looked after, several did not: six children stayed in the same placement throughout their time in care, and were expected to remain there until adulthood; ten others had only two placements. For them care offered protection and stability. The following chapters will explore further the factors that influenced these babies' experiences while they were looked after, and consider the complex relationship between instability and delay.

Points for practice

The findings from the study discussed in this chapter raise a number of important points that could lead to better evidence-based practice. In taking them into account it should, however, be noted that we were exploring the experiences of children who had already spent at least a year in care or accommodation; at this stage we do not know how their experiences compare with those of children in similar circumstances who were quickly reunited with their birth families, or who remained with them with the help of family support services. With this caveat, we can nevertheless draw the following conclusions:

- Social work decisions should be informed by accurate information concerning children's previous experience. Knowing how frequently children have changed address and carer *before* they become looked after can help social workers gauge the extent of instability in their lives and assess the probable strength of their attachments. Constant change prior to a care episode is an indicator of the fragility of a birth family that needs to be taken into account in making plans for the long-term future of very young children.

- Health problems, as well as emotional and behavioural difficulties that relate to previous experiences of instability and insecurity can mean that some very young children in care or accommodation have extensive needs.

- While the majority of children are best cared for within their family of origin, this is not true of *all* children. A long history of social services involvement, child neglect and abuse, problems associated with alcohol, drugs, mental illness and domestic violence should alert practitioners to the increased likelihood of family breakdown. Our evidence suggests that many very young children with such experiences will ultimately require a permanent home from outside the immediate family. The ability to recognise and act on such information would assist professionals not only to recognise those children who might be better placed for adoption, but also to speed up the adoption process and reduce delays.

- Very young children whose mothers have entrenched alcohol and/or drug problems are unlikely to be able to be reunited permanently with them within a realistic timeframe. On the other hand, very young children who have previously been at risk of significant harm are more likely to be permanently reunited with mothers who show little or no evidence of mental health, alcohol or drug problems and who have separated from a violent partner.

- The feasibility of a birth father providing a permanent home to a very young child following a lengthy care episode needs to be carefully assessed, particularly if he had not been living with the child at the time of admission. The evidence from what are admittedly a small number of cases in this study suggests that such placements can be fragile and may well require intensive family support.

Note

1   The definition of a placement is that used for the SSDA903 return, 1999, which required local authorities to report on all placements, including relief placements, if the duration was seven days or more. The definition has changed since these data were collected.

Chapter 3

Attachment and Loss

Experiences of Continuity against a Background of Constant Change

Introduction

One of the most significant issues so far identified by this study of very young children in care or accommodation has been the constant change that characterises so many of their lives. Chapter 2 demonstrated how many of the 42 babies studied had lived in chaotic households, with frequent changes of address and carer before they became looked after. It has also shown that many of these very young children experienced continuing instability after they entered care or accommodation: in the first twelve months, 17 had three or more placements, and in the second, six. This chapter explores the reasons for changes of placement while children were looked after, the resource issues that these reveal, and the opportunities that these very young children had for forming stable attachments against a background of constant change.

Reasons for changes of placement and carer while looked after

Ivaldi's (2000) survey of 1801 children adopted from local authority care in 1998–1999 found that 'infants aged 1 to 12 months were over-represented in the group of children with a complex history of care' (p.29). Many of the placement histories of the 42 babies we studied confirm this finding: only seven stayed in the same placement throughout their care episode. Taken together, the group as a whole experienced 143 placements[1] and 101 moves. Many first placements were extremely short – 12 were for one month or less, and 20 for less than six months – demonstrating their transient nature. Past research has tended to emphasise being older at placement and behavioural difficulties as key predictive factors in placement disruption and instability (see for example, Fratter *et al.* 1991; Hartnett *et al.* 1999). However, this study confirms Jackson and Thomas's (1999) conclusion that 'Contrary to the common view, changes of placement are as likely to be associated with service factors, as with the child's characteristics, background or behaviour' (p.43).

We have information about the reasons behind 100 of the 101 moves made by the 42 babies in our study. These are shown in Table 3.1 and are now explored to shed further light on the instability which is such a worrying feature of the care system.

Table 3.1: Reasons for placement change for 42 children while looked after

Reason for change	Percentage of moves (n=100)
Planned transitions	
Planned move to new placement	59
Foster carers need relief	8
Child ceased to be looked after	8
Unplanned transitions	
Placement no longer available	4
Residential assessment broke down	5
Placement with parent broke down	7
Placement with relatives/friends broke down	5
Placement with local authority foster carers broke down	4
Total	100
Not known	1

Unplanned changes of placement

One in four (25) of these 100 moves were unplanned transitions, made because placements ended prematurely. Four unplanned transitions occurred because a change in the carer's circumstances such as unexpected pregnancy, illness or sudden bereavement, meant that the placement was withdrawn. However 21 placements broke down, 17 with parents or relatives and 4 with local authority foster carers. Some of these very young children experienced more than one premature and unplanned change. There was insufficient information available in case-files to enable us to explore how far placements might have been strengthened by improved support to parents and carers.

The Children Act 1989 requires councils to:

(a) safeguard and promote the welfare of children within their area who are in need; and

(b) so far as is consistent with that duty, to promote the upbringing of such children by their families

(Section 17.1)

There is substantial evidence from this study that local authorities were making considerable efforts to promote the upbringing of children with their families, placing them wherever possible with own parents or with friends and relatives. However such arrangements were often fragile. It will be remembered that ten children eventually returned to their mothers or to both parents, and four to previously non-resident birth fathers. Some of these children had moved frequently between carers before permanence was achieved – and, as we have seen, a number continued to move after they had ceased to be looked after. In the early stages of the care episode attempts were also made to place eight other children with parents. Seven of these placements broke down, and one ended for other reasons. The placements tended to break down because parents were not providing satisfactory care or were finding it impossible to cope.

Ten babies were placed with their parents in residential assessment centres, where parenting capacity and attachment behaviour could be explored, and where parenting skills could be taught. However a shortage of places meant that there could be a long wait, and also that the child and parent could be placed out of the authority. Many of the parents were very young and vulnerable. They were removed from familiar surroundings and away from family support, as relatives sometimes could not visit because of the distance and cost involved. Half of these placements ended prematurely, for reasons such as those in Samantha's case.

Samantha's case

Samantha was placed in a residential assessment unit with her mother, who absconded because she found it difficult being away from her friends and family. Following discussions with her social worker, the mother agreed to go back, but on her return restrictions were introduced that included a reduction in the frequency of visits from family and friends – the main reason for her leaving in the first place. Shortly after this she left the unit, resumed her relationship with her ex-partner – a violent Schedule One offender – and Samantha was placed in foster care and subsequently adopted.

Placements in residential units could be very useful and often reduced the delay in finding a permanent solution. The opportunity to care for the child in a staffed and supportive environment while the assessment was conducted could promote bonding and helped some mothers to keep their babies. Nevertheless, a number of these assessments were undertaken in the expectation that the report would be negative, a point further explored in Chapter 4. A children's guardian commented:

> On paper it looks very expensive, but in practice, you know, it's an effective way of getting the evidence you might not have from other sources, [in one case] the court ordered a residential assessment and within a week the residential assessment had provided all the evidence that was required to make a clear decision…otherwise the case would have dragged on for ages. (Children's guardian)

Such placements could be extremely disruptive for the children concerned, particularly if a place only became available after the child had settled with new carers and then subsequently broke down. Moreover the assessment report did not necessarily determine the outcome of the case – one placement with parents disrupted after they had been assessed as capable of providing satisfactory care; another child was placed with a father who had had a positive assessment, but then moved to a mother who had been negatively assessed.

Five placements with relatives and family friends also ended unexpectedly. Two of these were because the relatives could not cope or were not thought to be meeting the children's needs; however others ended at their request – one because an aunt wanted to go back to work, and another because of the impact of the placement on other children in the household.

A placement with a family friend ended because she had not been made aware that the baby's mother would be living in her home for the duration of her assessment. This is similar to the reasons given for premature placement endings with two local authority foster carers: one was unable to sustain the level of assessed contact with birth parents, the other felt unable to maintain the placement as she experienced considerable hostility from the child's birth mother.

In three other cases the actions of birth parents increased the number of unexpected changes their babies experienced. One mother abducted the child during a contact visit. In a further two cases, birth parents formally requested the termination of foster placements; once because siblings had been separated owing to a shortage of placements for larger family groups, and once because of the standards of hygiene and cleanliness in the foster home. The extent to which the actions of birth parents influence children's pathways through care or accommodation is discussed further in Chapter 4.

One of the questions we wanted to answer in undertaking this study was why placements of very young children should have broken down. It is clear that the reasons had far more to do with the adults involved than the children concerned. Placements with parents were often part of the process by which the local authorities reached a decision as to their capacity to provide adequate care; their breakdown provided confirmation that permanence would need to be sought elsewhere. Placements with relatives were more likely to break down when families, who were often in difficult circumstances themselves, discovered the implications of providing long-term care for extra children. Some of the placement disruptions both with family and friends and with local authority foster carers can be regarded as evidence of the type of pressure placed on carers as they seek to implement policies that require them to work closely and in partnership with birth parents. There are obvious tensions when children are placed with members of an extended family. However these also occur when local authority foster carers are trying to work in partnership, for although in the best interests of the child, this can be an extremely difficult task, particularly if insufficient support is provided (see Poirier *et al.* forthcoming).

Planned changes of placement

While unplanned changes are likely to be disruptive and difficult for all concerned, they only account for a minority of moves. The most common reason given for changing placement was a 'planned transition', accounting for three quarters of all moves. However where such very young children are concerned, planned moves can increase their sense of unpredictability and instability and make it harder for them to develop secure attachments.

The incidence of planned transitions is likely to reflect a number of different factors. In eight cases babies experienced such a change, albeit temporarily, while foster carers went on holiday. Foster carers are a valuable resource. They undertake an extremely onerous task, often with relatively low remuneration: providing temporary respite placements so that they can have a break may be necessary in order to retain their services. However such placements are likely to be damaging to very young children, particularly given that most of the babies were placed with strangers during this time. The comment from May's adoptive mother (see Chapter 2) provides a graphic illustration of the long-term effects of frequent changes of this nature.

In three cases, however, it was clear that social services proactively sought to minimise the impact of such temporary moves. One child stayed with his grandparents, and two others were placed with their siblings' carers while their own foster carers went on holiday. In one of the latter cases the opportunity was taken to assess sibling relationships in order to decide whether they should be permanently placed together. In another case the foster carers' daughter moved back into the home and cared for the child while her parents were away. This provided the stability of familiar surroundings and a familiar carer for the child and also prevented any hiatus in the assessment of the birth parents. Providing the child has a positive relationship with temporary carers, such approaches can be viewed as valuable attempts to provide continuity and to minimise the damaging impact of instability and change.

Seven children had brief hospital admissions, which have not been included in the information on placement moves, as they would not have been recorded on the official returns. For those children who had suffered non-accidental head injuries or who had foetal alcohol syndrome these changes were, and will continue to be, a constant part of their lives, necessary to meet their complex health needs. It is important to note that despite the high level of movement experienced by these children, once looked after they tended to stay with one or two sets of foster carers and had fewer changes of placement than many of the other babies who did not have specialist health needs.

Four planned transitions were from short-term to long-term placements, indicating that appropriate placements could not always be found within the authorities at short notice. However by far the majority were positive planned moves, from foster care to permanent placements with relatives or parents, or to placements with adoptive families. Only eight of the babies moved placement when they ceased to be looked after.

Placing children from black and minority ethnic groups

A shortage of placements meant that it was not always possible to find carers who could meet children's needs. In all of the interviews with social services staff it was evident that their policy was to try and place black and minority ethnic children in similar cultural settings. However it could be difficult to find appropriate placements for children from minority groups, and there was an acknowledgement that, while same race placements might be desirable, they were often, in practice, almost impossible to achieve. This was partly due to a shortage of suitable foster carers from the various minority ethnic communities, but also the result of cultural diversity, mixed relationships, divorce and remarriage. In those local authorities where there were few, if any, black and minority ethnic children to place, one might have assumed that the problem would be more severe, but this did not seem to be the case. These authorities appeared to have managed to recruit a small number of foster carers from black and minority ethnic groups. The main shortages occurred in more culturally diverse areas:

> Same race [placement] is a problem; even if we have the same race carers, quite often you find that culturally, they may not have the same values and beliefs as the child's family... (Social worker)

> There are occasions when children aren't in same race placements...it's a real issue for me around dual heritage kids. What is a same race placement...if we have an Asian white child, we look for an Asian placement. So we could meet half their cultural needs...you could argue that a white placement meets half their [needs], but in [local authority] we don't do that... (Team leader)

> We have a child who's clearly mixed heritage, but has never experienced anything other than a white working class background...what sort of placement do you look for, for a child like that?... Nothing in her background, culturally, has any connection with Sierra Leone, but clearly in terms of her ethnic origins, future issues about her race and what have you, clearly it is an issue. But it's a balance isn't it? (Children's guardian)

One of the issues raised in interviews was that in the past, some had viewed same race placements as a 'politically correct' action and the ability of social workers to act in the best interests of the child had been questioned:

> Historically there was a period when it got people being dogmatic about issues around race, to the detriment of children again, without looking at the broader context. (Children's guardian)

The same debate continues around 'matching' children culturally and racially:

> Sometimes it looks to us as if they're doing a colour-coding thing. And that's from foster placement right through to adoptive...sometimes I

think it's very unhelpful, you know if you're looking at children who perhaps have a white mother, and, who was doing the caring, and say an Asian father who was never on the scene…parts of the child's upbringing whose culture had no influence on the child, when that child comes to placement, you know, the local authority are looking for, either a mixed race placement, or an Asian placement. (Children's guardian)

We became far too simple minded about it…had to be same race placement…spent too long trying to find the right same race placement…there were times when it was the only matching criteria. The same colour so they'll do it, irrespective of any other issues. (Team leader)

Our findings suggest that, while professionals attempted to find the best matches for children along racial and cultural lines, they also had some doubts themselves about what really is in the best interests of the child. The future need for an awareness of one's heritage and culture has to be balanced against the immediate need for a safe, secure and permanent home. Some social workers felt that ethnicity was less important than security for those children who would have had a white working-class upbringing, had they been left in their family of origin.

Ivaldi (2000) found no significant variation in the numbers of placements experienced by children from different ethnic groups (p.29). The numbers in our study are too small for formal statistical analysis. However, we found that, on average, babies from minority ethnic groups experienced slightly more placements over the care episode than did the white British children (3.8: 3.1), possibly because the former were more often moved from inappropriate placements when more appropriate ones became available. There is also evidence from our study that a shortage of appropriate adoptive placements meant that the very young children of dual or multiple heritage had to wait longer for a match: only one out of five of these babies (and 10 out of 13 white infants) was matched with appropriate adoptive parents within six months of a best interests decision being made.

Sibling groups

Of the 42 babies, 28 had siblings who were also looked after; eight had three or more, although not all siblings were admitted to care together.

Almost all of the professionals interviewed stated that policy within their department was to place sibling groups together wherever possible, unless there were serious contra-indications. However, in reality, most considered that sibling groups larger than three, or in many cases two, would be difficult to place. Once again, this was due to a shortage of appropriate foster carers. Although, again, the numbers are very small, there is some evidence to suggest that babies with siblings in care or accommodation had more moves than those without: 7 out of 28 of the former had only one or two placements in comparison with 7 out of 13 of the latter. However, in many cases these moves could be regarded as beneficial, for the purpose was often to reunite children who had previously been separated.

Matt's life pathway (see Chapter 4) demonstrates how children might be separated in one placement and then brought back together in another, as does Sara's experience, below.

Sara's case

Sara initially was taken into local authority care on her own, at seven months of age, without her half-brother. Sara's mother had been neglecting both children and failing to take Sara to medical appointments. Both children were often left in the care of others and, in Sara's case, the alternative carers were considered inappropriate. A full family assessment by social services and a specialist report by an adult psychologist concluded that both children needed a permanent home and that their mother was unable to meet the needs of either in the long term. Sara's brother joined her in the foster home when Sara was 14 months old and both children were placed together with potential adopters when Sara was two. During the time that they were apart, contact was facilitated by social workers.

In some cases, where there were no foster carers available, other options had been explored to maintain sibling groups:

> We did re-open a children's home and put five or six children [siblings] in that with staff to keep them together. (Social worker)

In another case, a group of four siblings were separated between two families: one full and one half sibling were placed together in each of them – a decision based on observation of sibling dynamics. Other social workers indicated that larger sibling groups might have to be placed out of area, in another local authority, if they were to be kept together. This would then necessitate using scarce resources in order to maintain contact between siblings and birth families. Such decisions, based on an under-standing of the best interests of the child, could have considerable resource implications.

Social workers were clear in their reasons for trying to maintain sibling groups:

> I personally think it's important if it's at all possible for siblings to stay together because of a sense of identity that the children need. (Social worker)

> Sibling attachment tends to be one of the longest relationships people have. (Social worker)

However many professionals recognised that it was sometimes necessary to separate sibling groups:

> There are justifiable reasons for separating sibling groups, issues around sexual abuse and things like that...in the best interest and not just led by resources or convenience. (Social worker)

> Sibling groups usually needed to be divided, but it is also about the individual needs of children that have to be considered. Again, choice was not always available. (Social worker)

Practitioners were relatively successful at maintaining family groups. There is evidence that many siblings, who were separated at admission or in early placements, were later reunited. Eight of the 28 babies who had siblings who were also looked after were placed with one or more of them at admission. By the time they ceased to be looked after, 18 were placed together – a substantial achievement.

However there is evidence from this and other studies (see for example Ivaldi 2000) that attempts to keep sibling groups together contributed substantially to delays in the process of achieving permanence. Only two of the babies placed with siblings were matched with prospective adoptive families within six months of the best interests decision being made. Where sibling groups were black or of dual or multiple heritage the delays were particularly protracted. It is a matter of concern that, because of these and other delays, some of the babies were old enough to fall into the 'difficult to place' category by the time they achieved permanence.

Whelan (2003) suggests that:

> There are situations in which social workers must temper their drive to maintain family unity and accept that separation of family members can be in the best interests of the child. (p.22)

Better information about the likelihood of finding placements for sibling groups might have made it easier to make such decisions more quickly. As the study of the full cohort demonstrates, information about what has been possible in the past can be used to inform future decision-making (Ward *et al.* forthcoming a). However, the following comments show that deciding how to separate families involves difficult and painful decisions:

> The thing was, if we'd split them [siblings] up we might have got some of the young ones, or younger two adopted. (Social worker)

> From instances before when there was a group of five [siblings], you'll find that one of the children will remain with her father, the baby will go to adoption on their own, the middle two will go together and the eldest will go separately. (Social worker)

> [Relative care] allowed the children to stay together which, because of the very big age difference, if they were a looked after child coming into a care situation, it probably would have been that [the youngest] would have been adopted separately, away from her brother. And her brother's always been really close to her. I think that would have been quite a devastating effect on him really. (Social worker)

In the comment above there was obviously a strong attachment between the two siblings. Where close relationships have evolved, foster placements with siblings can provide support and continuity during a period of change and loss. However the strength of sibling attachments between vulnerable children cannot always be taken for granted. There is some evidence to suggest that the bond can be particularly strong where children have grown up in families in which parents have been unable to provide adequate care or protection (Ainsworth 1989; Ward forthcoming). On the other hand, however, many vulnerable children come from families where parental attention is at a premium, where siblings have had little previous contact and where rivalry may be high. The strength of sibling attachments in vulnerable families is an area that would benefit from further research.

Many of the babies came from reconstituted families; apparently close relationships had evolved between half- and step-siblings, as well as between children with the same parents. In many instances half-siblings were of different racial heritage. However, in spite of the complexity of these issues and the difficulties associated with placing large groups together, in only three cases was a psychological assessment of sibling relationships undertaken. In the first case, two older siblings had complex needs and behavioural difficulties; in the second, a sibling group had been separated when they entered foster care and there was uncertainty as to whether it would be viable to place them permanently together, given that they were of multiple heritage, one was considerably older than the others, and they were all boys (older boys being difficult to place). It is noteworthy that in one of these cases the issue was only raised after it became evident that there would be delays in finding permanent placements for the whole family. In the third case the court ordered a psychological assessment of sibling relationships. This court direction, at the point of freeing, led to further delay in the child being adopted.

The findings suggest that, while policy dictates that sibling groups should be placed together, practice often falls short of this aim, because of a lack of resources. Once this happens, other factors such as the closeness of the siblings, the individual child's interests and the best interests of the majority take priority. Babies, by virtue of their age, have the greatest chance of finding permanent adoptive placements. However, this is sometimes at the expense of their sibling relationships. Matt's case (see Chapter 4) demonstrates how babies and younger children may gain in the adoption stakes but miss out on the stability of established sibling relationships.

Only half of those babies who were adopted and had siblings were placed with them. In at least two of these cases complex health needs meant that placement with siblings was not considered to be in the child's best interest.

It is also noteworthy that, in cases where older siblings were already permanently placed, it was rare for professionals to consider the viability of placing younger siblings with them. In these cases, direct contact was also less likely to be established.

> We have a significant number of siblings who were born subsequently, so they've never lived with their other sibling…in those cases it might just be…indirect contact. (Family placement worker)

This could mean that, even when siblings expressed a desire to meet their younger brothers or sisters, this was not facilitated by social services. The rationale was that the stability of the placements might be undermined, particularly if older siblings were placed with relatives and maintained contact with their birth parent(s) while the care plan for the youngest sibling was adoption.

Implications of a shortage of foster carers

Many of the professionals interviewed acknowledged that a shortage of foster carers was a major resource issue. We have already seen that insufficient numbers of placements, particularly for children from black and minority ethnic groups or of multiple heritage and for large sibling groups, increased the chances of these very young children experiencing continued instability while they were looked after by the local authorities; this also increased the delay before they were likely to achieve permanence. One of the issues that raised the greatest concerns was that, at the time that this study was undertaken, some foster carers were discouraged from adopting children for fear that the authority would lose their services:

> I don't know whether you would call it policy, but I think we were certainly – we being social workers or locality workers – were discouraged

from raising that [adoption by foster carers] as an issue, it seemed to me because we had a paucity of carers at that particular time. (Social worker)

This meant that some children, who had already had frequent experiences of loss and change in their lives, developed attachments to foster carers but then were required to move on to other adoptive families for permanent placement. It also meant that there were additional delays in achieving permanence for some children. Six babies spent between 14 and 24 months with foster carers before they were permanently placed with adoptive families.

Children were moved on to new placements for adoption not only because of concerns that a valuable resource would otherwise be lost but also because of suspicion about the motives of foster carers who applied to be considered. One of the children's guardians explained that foster carers had not been assessed as potential adopters and that many would *not* be considered as such. Although the criteria for becoming adoptive parents and foster carers may differ, both have to be approved by panels and have an assessment, references, Criminal Records Bureau disclosures and so on (Department of Health 2002).

Furthermore, the National Adoption Standards (Department of Health 2001b) state that:

Foster carers who make a formal application to adopt children in their care will be entitled to the same information and preparation as other adopters and be assessed within four months. (Department of Health 2001b, B5)

The Children Act 1989 Guidance and Regulations (Department of Health 1991) make it clear that different standards might come into play when approving relatives and family friends as foster carers. However, it also appears that different standards of approval might operate between foster carers and potential adopters. Concerns should be raised as to why some foster carers should be regarded as suitable to look after children for several weeks, months and, in some cases years, if they are not deemed suitable to care for them on a permanent basis.

Although some professionals expressed reservations about foster carers adopting, others identified clear benefits:

> I think some professionals get a bit alarmed about where the foster carer's coming from…it's unnecessarily sort of doubting the motives of the foster carer. The fact is that she's attached…she and the child have got a great relationship…her other kids love the kid to death…what's complicated about that? (Social worker)

Three of the babies were eventually adopted by their foster carers. These children therefore remained with carers whom they had known and lived with for the majority of their short lives and to whom they had formed attachments. In a further three cases foster carers considered applying to adopt but did not pursue this. In one case they were not considered to be an ethnic match; in the second they were considered to be too old and one of them was found to have committed a Schedule One offence several years earlier. Both of the children in these cases had been placed with their foster carers at one month old; the first had remained with them until aged 16 months, the second until after his first birthday. In the second case, where age was cited as one of the reasons not to approve the foster carers, an older couple eventually adopted the child. Both children had formed strong attachments to their foster carers before being moved to permanent homes.

In the third case the foster carers decided not to pursue adoption of a child with complex health needs, the result of a non-accidental injury:

> Right from the beginning the plan was for [foster carer] to adopt Kathryn, however she withdrew for a number of reasons…there were various things she wasn't happy with and a feeling that she'd lose support from social services if she went down that route. (Social worker)

The perceived lack of post-adoption support was one reason why Kathryn was not adopted. However, the National Adoption Standards do now acknowledge that adoptive parents 'Will have access to a range of multi-agency support services before, during and after adoption. Support services will include practical help, professional advice, and financial assistance where needed' (Department of Health 2001b, C3).

New government policies, which create incentives to increase the proportion of children placed for adoption, are likely to mean that local authorities will be less likely to discourage foster carers from applying to adopt children who have been placed with them.

It was clear from the interviews that all local authorities experienced not only shortages of foster carers, but also of adoptive carers. After exhausting local resources, some used adoption consortia, while others made attempts on a national basis, via 'Find a Family', or similar schemes, to try to match children with prospective adopters. There was a tacit acknowledgement that there is not an inexhaustible pool of potential alternative carers just waiting to be accessed. As one social worker commented:

> We're getting to the bottom of what is available...there aren't more families to find who are suitable, and therefore we are having to compromise more in the sorts of decisions we are making. (Social worker)

While the new legislation aims to speed up the process of adoption, success will continue to depend on local authorities and other agencies recruiting sufficient numbers of suitable carers. It will be important to ensure that this selection process is not compromised and that the need for faster routes to permanence is balanced by the need for high quality carers. In terms of future policy and practice, if permanence is to be achieved more quickly, foster carers cannot on the one hand be deemed such an important resource that they must not be lost while, at the same time, being considered only suitable as providers of temporary care.

Mitigating the effects of constant change

A number of studies have shown how, as children move between placements and carers, key figures become lost (see Jackson and Thomas 1999; Millham *et al.* 1986; Skuse and Ward 2003). We have already seen how sibling groups were sometimes split in order to improve children's chances of securing permanent placements. Further evidence from the wider study from which these babies were drawn shows that treasured possessions were often lost as children moved from one placement to another, and that a number of young people lost touch with parents, relations and former carers (see Skuse and Ward 2003).

However our study shows that, with these very young children, substantial efforts were made to mitigate the effects of separation and change by promoting and maintaining sibling relationships and contacts with birth parents. Our findings confirm those of Cleaver (2000) that such arrangements can be extremely onerous and time-consuming; some of the children's experiences also demonstrate the dangers of assuming that such arrangements will automatically be in their best interests.

Contact with siblings

In many families where parents separate, children may not live together but contact often continues. The same was true for some of the sibling groups in this study, where it was evident that, when separate placements had to be found, professionals went to considerable lengths to maintain sibling contact if it was thought to be in the children's interests. Contact was an additional factor that had to be facilitated by social services staff and therefore local placements that met children's needs were considered the best option to save time and money – both valuable resources. Contact would sometimes be facilitated as part of a plan to reunite a sibling group in the long term:

> If we can't [keep sibling groups together], what we do arrange is sibling contact on a regular basis and look to them joining each other later on. (Social worker)

However contact could also continue when children had been adopted separately. Such arrangements were based on individual cases and could work well:

> If we had a large sibling group I think that we would feel reasonably comfortable in splitting them in order to place them and ensuring that the children meet… I've been involved in the placing of a number of sibling groups and one might have happened four, five years ago, where I know that once a year they're all meeting and spending a week in each other's homes. (Social worker)

Nevertheless such contact was not always regarded as beneficial to all the children concerned. In Carly's case contact did not appear to be in the interests of one of her half-brothers; his reluctance to participate led to the adoptive carers feeling rejected and this was eventually perceived as having destroyed the sibling relationship.

CARLY'S CASE

Carly was initially placed with her full sibling, while her two half-siblings were placed elsewhere. A decision was then taken to place all the children permanently and prospective adopters were identified who were prepared to take all four. However, one of Carly's half-siblings did not settle well in the placement. Rather than compromise the adoption for the remaining children, this child was removed to different foster carers. Although contact between the siblings began, it broke down because the half-sibling did not want to continue visiting. The potential adopters, in turn, felt rejected by the child and relations between them and the other foster carers deteriorated. One family adopted Carly and her two siblings and another adopted her half-sibling. Because of the previous problems, Carly and her two siblings ceased to have contact with their brother. Although they lived in the same town and still saw one another, the adoptive parents actively discouraged the children from speaking to their brother. In this case, the best interests of the majority outweighed other considerations as none of the parties involved wished to see the adoption break down.

Contact with birth parents

Considerable efforts were also made to maintain contact with birth parents. Parents tended to be either taken to the foster carers' homes or to family centres if contact had to be supervised or distance was an issue. Such arrangements consume a substantial amount of resources as social workers often accompany families – birth parents, siblings and important others – to contact meetings (see Cleaver 2000). Such contact visits can also cause conflict between birth parents and foster carers:

> I think there's been a bit of an issue around actually saying to foster carers, 'I'm sorry, you know, contact has to take place…I fully accept that,

your child when she returns throws a wobbler...we need to try and understand why...support the child through it. To say that a child should not have contact, purely because you as a foster carer can't cope with it isn't on. (Social worker)

Conflicts such as these can make parents, carers and children all feel threatened. Contact arrangements between parents and very small children can also be extremely time-consuming, particularly if the aim is to support frequent interactions in order to strengthen attachments. We have already seen that three foster placements disrupted because carers felt that the demands of sustaining contacts between child and birth mother were excessive. How carers can be better supported to sustain contacts is an issue that warrants further attention.

If children are to be adopted, the issue of contact with birth parents becomes more complex. Before a full care order is made, courts are unlikely to stop contact between birth parent(s) and children, so up to that point social workers may be maintaining relationships that they anticipate will ultimately be terminated. It was clear that in a number of cases social workers felt that contact was detrimental to the child, but were reluctant to reduce it and pre-empt court decisions. Five of the babies spent a year or longer in the care system before a final care order was granted. In two of these cases protracted contact was maintained, in spite of the expectation that the babies would eventually be freed for adoption. In Beth's case (see Chapters 1 and 2) a decision had been delayed to allow further assessment of the extent to which the child's mother had addressed her drug addiction. The mother's solicitor also requested a psychiatric report. The assessment could not be completed immediately and further delays were encountered because Beth's mother failed to attend arranged meetings. It was anticipated that at the final hearing for the care order Beth would be simultaneously freed. However, the judge did not grant the freeing order. The local authority successfully appealed against this decision, but on the basis of the judgement her mother's solicitor requested that contact should be maintained at current levels until the appeal hearing. Contact was therefore maintained for a further two months until the freeing order was granted, by which time Beth was aged 25 months and had been placed away from home for 14 of them.

Where one child from a family was placed with potential adopters and there was no expectation of a continuing relationship with birth parents, contact with siblings might also be terminated if they were living in the parental home:

> Security of placement...if you end up with kids, some of the older children, perhaps having some sort of contact with natural family, but the younger children perhaps being placed for adoption, and it becomes very difficult to balance the needs of different children. (Social worker)

In these cases, the best interests of the child and their right to see siblings had to be balanced against any potential disruption to the placement that might result from birth parents tracing adopted children. Adoptive parents sometimes prevented contact between siblings, partly because they were afraid of losing the children or had concerns about birth parents tracing them.

The National Adoption Standards state that:

> Where it is in the child's best interest for there to be ongoing links, including contact, with birth parents and families (including siblings separated by adoption), birth families will be involved in discussions about how best to achieve this and helped to fulfil agreed plans, e.g. through practical or financial support. (Department of Health 2001b, D7)

Although such contact can be assumed to be a child's right, it is rarely followed up after adoption:

> Adoption is a different situation really. We ask that adopters keep some contact, even if it's not face-to-face contact, through the post box system update. Trouble is that once they're adopted, you've got no control over what they do...the court can make as many orders as they like, in the adoption, but really they can only make an adoption order. (Social worker)

Information drawn from interviews with carers and older children in the wider study of 242 children suggested that the post box system (whereby letters can be exchanged between adoptive carers and birth parents giving information about the children) provided only a very tenuous link between adopted children and birth parents. Carers who wrote an annual letter to birth parents about a child's progress claimed that they were rarely told if it had been received (Skuse and Ward 2003). Where the babies were concerned it appeared that some adoptive parents were also reluctant to pursue the relationship:

> When the Children Act 1989 came out there was this whole idea...[that it] would be more important [to] maintain contact with the family of origin...[now it's] slipped back to your adopters don't want contact with your natural family... And certainly adoption agencies talk about 'Well my adopters wouldn't like this', and the judges haven't been making contact orders. (Social worker)

Professionals are, yet again, left balancing the competing needs of children for permanence against their need to maintain continuity and contact with their family of origin.

Conclusion

The children were subject to a surprising amount of change, not only before they became looked after, but also after entry to care or accommodation. One in four moves in care was an unplanned transition, most of them resulting from the breakdown of placements with parents, relatives or foster carers. There is no evidence that such breakdowns were engendered by the behaviour patterns of these very small children – though many may have been demanding and difficult to care for. Rather, breakdowns were due to the difficulties parents had in providing adequate care or to the pressures placed on relative or local authority foster carers. However the majority of moves were more positive, as children moved from temporary arrangements to permanent placements. Limited resources meant that some sibling groups were split, and some foster carers were discouraged from applying to adopt. While attempts were made to provide some continuity for children who were unavoidably separated from key figures, contacts were sometimes artificially protracted while decisions about permanence were made.

Points for practice

Findings discussed in this chapter raise further points that could lead to better evidence-based practice:

- Even very young children can experience numerous moves while looked after by local authorities, and such experiences are likely to prove detrimental to their ability to develop attachments. Stability may be increased by assessing parenting capacity at a very early stage; avoiding placements with birth parents where the purpose is to gather evidence of incapacity; and ensuring that babies are not placed with foster carers who are about to go on holiday.

- Arrangements to place very young children with birth parents in residential assessment units can be problematic. Such placements often only become available after children have settled with foster carers, and may therefore be a cause of instability. They also tend to separate very young parents from support networks; half of those used in this study broke down, largely because parents found it difficult to cope with the isolation. Although such placements can be very useful in providing a speedy assessment that reduces delays in decision-making, their disadvantages need to be taken into account.

- While ethnicity is an important consideration, it is often only one of many. Finding a perfectly matched placement for children of dual or multiple heritage may prove impossible, and will be rendered even more complex if there are siblings of different ethnicity. There is a complex inter-relationship between delay and instability, and some children become 'hard to place' while they wait for the right match. There may come a point when the need to achieve a permanent, stable placement for a child has to over-ride all other considerations.

- This study found that assessments of sibling attachments were rare, and often only undertaken at a late stage in the process of finding permanent placements. Earlier assessments would provide better evidence on which to base difficult decisions about placing siblings together or separately.

- Decisions about how long to wait for same race placements or for placements for sibling groups might also be informed by making better use of evidence concerning what the agency has been able to achieve in the past. Recent changes, such as a recruitment drive for foster carers from ethnic minority groups, could still be put forward as factors likely to increase capacity, although their impact would need to be evaluated.

- Foster carers and relatives need adequate support if they are to work in partnership with birth parents, who may be demanding or hostile. Inadequate preparation for this role, and insufficient clarity about the extent and nature of parental contact were factors in some placement disruptions.

- Different thresholds of approval may operate between relative carers, local authority foster carers and potential adoptive parents, although all may be expected to meet children's needs. Some agencies may need to question practices that deem foster carers suitable to look after children for months or years, but not on a permanent basis.

Note

1   The definition of a placement is that used for the SSDA return, 1999, which required local authorities to report on all placements, including relief placements, if the duration was seven days or more. The definition has changed since these data were collected.

Chapter 4

Permanence

Why Did It Take So Long to Achieve?

Introduction

By the end of the study discussed in this book, between five and six years
after they had entered care or accommodation, all the 42 babies were
placed with carers who were expected to look after them until adulthood,
although three were still officially in the care of a local authority. We have
seen, however, that for many of them, achieving a degree of stability and
permanence had been a lengthy process, and there were numerous
experiences of change and loss on the way.

A number of studies demonstrate the adverse effects of delay, instability and impermanence on children's life pathways (see, for example, Howe
2001; Quinton *et al.* 1998; Rutter, Quinton and Hill 1990). Lowe and
Murch (2002) emphasise the importance of remembering that babies and
infants have a different concept of time from adults and are therefore less
able to tolerate uncertainty and delay. Jackson and Thomas (1999) suggest
that delay in finding permanent families for neglected or abused babies is
associated with less satisfactory outcomes:

> Coming from chaotic backgrounds, too many enter a system which
> inflicts further damage on their social, emotional and cognitive develop-
> ment by its failure to provide a place where they can be confident of
> staying for any length of time. (p.4)

We have already seen (Chapter 2) that some of the children in this study
were still showing signs of emotional and behavioural difficulty when

their carers were interviewed in 2002–2003, between five and six years after they had entered care or accommodation.

So far we have considered the reasons why these very young children were placed in care or accommodation, and we have explored their life pathways from birth through care to final placement with adoptive families or relatives and the factors associated with change and continuity. This chapter seeks to discover why the process of achieving permanence took so long and why there were so many very young children in this situation.

Timeframes from entry to permanence

On the face of it, it appears that the babies in this study spent a very long time looked after by the authorities. As we already know, all of them had spent at least a year in care or accommodation. Table 4.1 shows the length of time the children were looked after, comparing those who were adopted with those who were eventually placed permanently with parents or other relatives. Information about the exact length of care episodes was available for 38 of the 42 babies: 16 were looked after for between 12 and 24 months; 11 between two and three years and 11 for longer than three years, three of these for more than five years. On average, children who were placed for adoption spent fewer months (29) looked after than those who were eventually rehabilitated with family members (34 months).

Concerns have been raised about the extent to which children's care pathways are subject to unnecessary delays. Delays are considered to be detrimental, both because they are costly to the authorities and also because they are likely to indicate that children are drifting in the care system, without proper plans being implemented for their long-term well-being. The frequent changes of placement and carer explored in Chapter 3, all occurred in the period before the babies achieved permanence; it is evident that the longer they spent in limbo, waiting to find a final home, the more likely they were to experience further change and loss.

However one should, perhaps, begin by asking at what point permanence had been reached, for it quickly became evident that many of the babies had been securely placed well before their legal position was

Table 4.1: Months the children were looked after by eventual outcome

Months looked after	Placement outcome (n=38)	
	Adoption	Living with parents or relatives
0–6	0	0
7–12	0	0
13–18	4	4
19–24	5	3
25–30	6	2
31–36	2	1
>36	5	6
Total	22	16

Missing data: complete missing data in one case; date of one adoption order; two children still looked after.

finalised. From a very young child's perspective it could be argued that long-term stability and continuity of placement and carer were of greater importance than legal permanence via, for example, an adoption or a residence order. Indeed, as we shall see, some children were deliberately kept in care after they had found a permanent placement so that they might continue to be protected.

We collected information both on the length of time children were looked after and on timeframes from entry until they moved to the home in which they would permanently remain. Table 4.2 shows the timeframes from entry to reaching their permanent home for the 41 children for whom information was available.

Table 4.2: Months from entering care to the children reaching a permanent home

Months to permanence	Placement outcome (n=41)	
	Adoption	*Living with parents or relatives*
0–6	4	5
7–12	6	3
13–18	6	4
19–24	4	3
25–30	0	1
31–36	2	2
>36	1	0
Total	23	18

Overall, 10 of the 23 babies placed for adoption reached their permanent home within one year. A slightly lower proportion, 8 out of 18, of those babies placed with parents or relatives achieved permanence within this timeframe. Two years after entry a slightly higher proportion of children placed for adoption had achieved permanence (20 out of 23), compared with those who returned to parents or relatives (15 out of 18). The two children who were still looked after at the end of the study period were both placed with relatives and would leave care as soon as a residence order had been granted; they had achieved permanence within 10 and 29 months respectively. *On average*, children who were placed for adoption spent 15 months in the care system before permanence was achieved; this was one month longer than the average length of care before permanent placement for those who were eventually rehabilitated (14 months). *On average*, children who returned to birth parents tended to find a permanent placement within a slightly shorter timeframe, but they tended to remain the responsibility of the local authority for longer.

Timeframes to permanence for children placed with family

Timeframes from entry to permanence for babies who returned to parents or relatives ranged from zero to 36 months. Two were committed to the care of the local authority but placed with their mothers from birth, as was one who was placed immediately with a grandparent. From the babies' perspectives these had always been their permanent homes; from an administrative perspective, however, the children remained looked after for five years or longer. In the case below, delay was positive and deliberate and served to protect Hayley while her home situation stabilised.

Hayley's case

Before she was born, Hayley's father had assaulted her half-brothers, Ben and Mike and her mother had failed to protect them from significant harm. At the time of Hayley's birth, her two brothers were placed with foster carers and the father had left the family home. At birth Hayley was placed with her mother on an interim care order; the situation was assessed and support offered. When she was three months old, Hayley and her mother moved in with an uncle who often had to prompt her mother to meet her needs. However, eight months later Hayley's mother had secured her own tenancy and consideration was given to revoking the care order. By this time Hayley was 14 months old. She was closely attached to her mother whose caregiving had improved. Given the past history and the limited time Hayley and her mother had lived independently it was felt to be too soon to revoke the care order. At subsequent reviews additional concerns were raised and revocation of the care order was purposely delayed. Contact issues needed to be addressed to prevent Hayley's father from undermining the stability and safety of the placement. Concerns were also expressed about the emotional harm Hayley suffered from the aggressive behaviour of one of her half-brothers. The care order was finally revoked when Hayley was five years old.

In this, as in other cases where these very young children were placed with parents, permanence might be achieved at an early stage, but social services involvement would persist until there was evidence that the child was adequately protected. Similar situations sometimes arose where children were permanently placed with relatives, but involvement persisted until a residence order had been obtained. Purposive delay of this nature can therefore be viewed as a positive factor.

Timeframes to permanence for children placed for adoption

Specific procedures have to be followed before children can be adopted (Adoption Act 1976; the Adoption Agencies and Children (Arrangements for Placements and Reviews (miscellaneous Amendments) Regulations 1997; Adoption Agency Regulations 1983; the Adoption (Amendment) Rules 1991; Adoption Rules 1984). The regulations require the Adoption Panel to agree that an adoption is in the child's best interests and then make a decision about the suitability of potential adopters and agree the match. Applications also have to be made to the court for freeing orders, to dispense with parents' consent to adoption and remove parental responsibility from them (Adoption Act 1976, Section 16).[1] Delays in achieving permanence could occur at each stage of this process; moreover difficulties in securing court time meant that any decision that had to be referred back to the courts could substantially extend the timeframe.

Four children achieved permanence via placement for adoption within six months. Two of these were placed immediately with carers who later adopted them, thus achieving physical and emotional permanence as soon as they were looked after. One other was similarly placed within three months. These had not been intended as long-term placements at the outset, but strong attachments had developed between the carers and children. In the fourth case delays engendered by court proceedings were avoided as the case was consolidated with ongoing care proceedings concerning an older brother (see Craig's case, below). On average, however, it took eight and a half months for care proceedings to be completed for children in this study; however there was a wide range from 2 to 22 months. In addition to care proceedings, a 'best interests' decision is also required, before a child can be matched with prospective adoptive parents. In the majority (15) of cases for which information was available, it took six months or more for this decision to be reached. In one case, a baby looked after from birth was 27 months old when a best interests decision was taken. This child did not find a permanent home until he was aged three years one month (see Appendix, Table A.6 for further details).

Following the best interests decision an appropriate prospective adoptive family needs to be identified and matched. The Adoption Standards state that where adoption is the plan 'A match with suitable adoptive parents will be identified and approved by panel within six months of the agency agreeing that adoption is in the child's best interests' (Department of Health 2001b, p.17).

Eleven of the babies were matched within six months of the best interests decision and seven were not. There was no information on the other five. The difficulties of finding suitable placements for children from minority ethnic groups or for siblings were explored in Chapter 3. Only one child of dual heritage and two children who were part of sibling groups were matched within the target timeframes.

The two timelines below show the longest and shortest timeframes between entry and permanence achieved for children who were eventually placed with prospective adoptive carers, excluding the three who were eventually adopted by their foster carers.

Craig and Dean's cases

Craig and Dean were both placed in the care of the local authority immediately after birth. Craig was initially accommodated under the Children Act 1989, Section 20. However his mother decided that she was not able to commit to caring for him and did not oppose the making of a care order. It was therefore possible to bring this application forward and consolidate it with proceedings in respect of his older brother. Craig was permanently placed with prospective adoptive carers at the age of six months, although he remained looked after for a further 11 months until the adoption order was granted.

In contrast Dean was not permanently placed until he was three years one month, and he then remained looked after for a further eight months. Although he was committed to the care of the local authority at six days old under an emergency protection order, following a residential

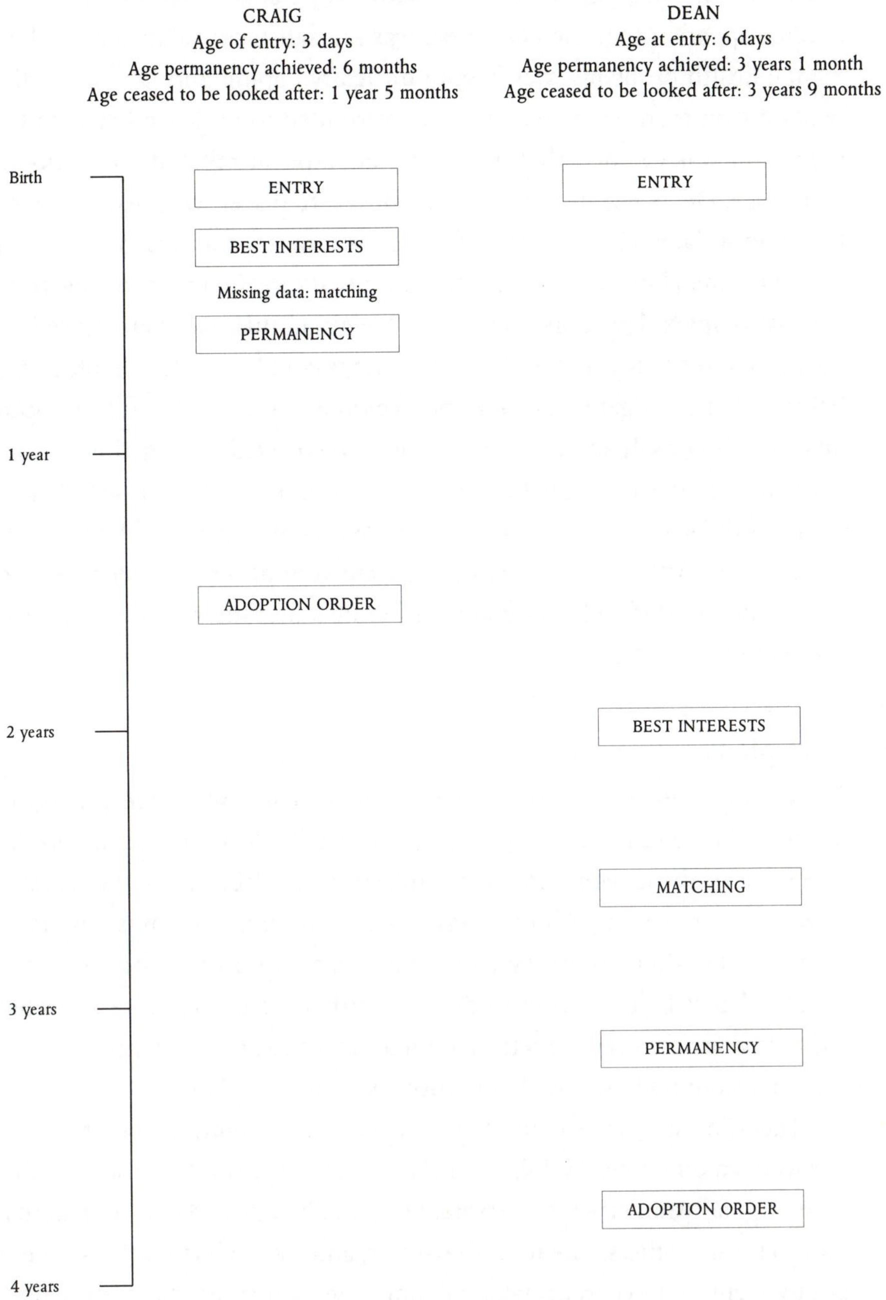

CRAIG
Age of entry: 3 days
Age permanency achieved: 6 months
Age ceased to be looked after: 1 year 5 months

DEAN
Age at entry: 6 days
Age permanency achieved: 3 years 1 month
Age ceased to be looked after: 3 years 9 months

Birth

| ENTRY |

| ENTRY |

| BEST INTERESTS |

Missing data: matching

| PERMANENCY |

1 year

| ADOPTION ORDER |

2 years

| BEST INTERESTS |

| MATCHING |

3 years

| PERMANENCY |

| ADOPTION ORDER |

4 years

Figure 4.1: Timeline of Craig and Dean's cases from entering care to adoption

assessment he was placed at home with his parents. After 17 months it became apparent that the placement was not satisfactory: his mother had mental health problems, was having difficulty coping and Dean was displaying disturbed behaviour that was attributed to violence between his parents. It was decided that no further attempts at rehabilitation should take place. Dean and his younger brother were placed with foster carers; two months later a best interests decision was taken, and five months later they were matched. The prospective adoptive carers were made aware of Dean's complex developmental needs. Delays in this case were caused by the need to test out whether the birth parents could provide a viable home before other arrangements could be explored. However Dean's development was adversely affected by the care he received during this period. Complex, contested legal proceedings and appeals also caused delays. While both Dean and Craig entered care or accommodation almost immediately after birth, their life pathways were very different. Indeed, Craig had already ceased to be looked after before a best interests decision was made in respect of Dean.

Care plans

Some indications as to why achieving permanence was such a lengthy business can be found in the planning process. Table 4.3 shows the initial care plans of those babies for whom data were available and demonstrates how these compared with the final outcome. At entry, the most common plan was time-limited assessment, considered appropriate for 17 of the babies, almost half of those studied. A further 14 babies were expected either to remain with or to return to their birth parents. Only three entered care or accommodation with adoption as their care plan.

Time-limited assessment is not a permanent solution, but rather a means to an outcome. As Table 4.3 also shows, only seven of those babies who originally underwent assessment eventually returned to birth parents: four to birth mothers, one to both parents, and two to birth fathers. These last two returned to parents who had not been living with them at the time of admission. As Table 4.3 shows, over half (9) of the babies admitted for time-limited assessment were eventually adopted.

Table 4.3: Initial care plan for the children compared with eventual outcome

| Initial care plan | Final outcome (n=39) | | | | | | |
	Adopted	Mother	Father	Both parents	Relatives	Looked after	Total
Time-limited assessment	9	4	2	1	0	1	17
Remain with family	1	2	1	0	0	1	5
Return to birth family	7	1	0	0	1	0	9
Relatives/friends	0	0	0	0	1	0	1
Long-term placement	0	0	0	0	0	1	1
Adoption	3	0	0	0	0	0	3
Other	1	1	0	1	0	0	3
Total	21	8	3	2	2	3	39

Data are missing on care plans for two adopted children and one who returned to birth father.

Similarly, plans for babies to remain with or return to their birth family were frequently unfulfilled: eight of the fourteen babies who had this as their initial care plan were later adopted. We have already seen (Chapter 3) that placements with parents frequently broke down. This is in line with findings from a study by Harwin and colleagues (2001), which showed that home placement had the lowest fulfilment rate of all placement types.

The only care plan at entry that was fulfilled in all cases was adoption. However, those babies who entered care or accommodation with this as their plan were still not guaranteed an easy pathway through the system (see for example Matt's case below).

Retrospectively, it appears care plans were often over-optimistic. The information from case-files and interviews sheds some light on why this might have been. It confirms that, both as a matter of policy and practice, rehabilitation to birth parents was considered to be the optimal outcome for most looked after children – the first choice wherever possible. The only reasons cited for not considering it a viable option were serious sexual abuse where the perpetrator remained in the child's usual residence, and other types of abuse where there was no acceptance of guilt or a gross failure to protect the child. Even where a child had been previously abused, rehabilitation was sometimes achieved, as the example of Natasha (later in this chapter) shows.

As earlier chapters have shown, for a number of the children rehabilitation was not a realistic option. However, because it was regarded as the optimal outcome, it often had to be tried before other plans could be considered. Doing so inevitably caused delays in achieving permanence. One of the children's guardians highlighted this:

> This case was in a particular [social work] team where they are known to – and I'm not saying this is a bad thing – but work extremely hard to exhaust all possibilities, which of course they should, with the mother. But this particular mother had been known as a child herself in care to all members of the team, and they had put in vast resources…they were almost overly committed to the mum really… (Children's guardian)

In this particular case the child was ultimately placed for adoption, but the long attempts at rehabilitation led to delay. This case also demonstrates how the practitioners' relationship with the mother, who had herself been a looked after child in the same authority, affected their decision-making. Where social workers have had continuing responsibility for a young woman who becomes a mother it is difficult to separate the parent's interests from those of the child.

Social workers were not the only professionals who regarded rehabilitation as the optimal outcome. In another case, where the social services department thought adoption was indicated, the children's guardian felt rehabilitation was achievable and went to great lengths to have the mother assessed and given support in order for this to happen:

> I was horrified myself [at the child's injuries] but it was the extent of talking to the mother, of really understanding her paralysis at not being able to protect this child... (Children's guardian)

In this case rehabilitation was achieved and at the final court hearing the care order was discharged.

Courts also, mindful of the implications of the Human Rights Act 1998, needed to be certain that parents were demonstrably unable to meet their children's needs before they would make orders that would limit their rights to 'respect for private and family life' (Article 8). In most cases the chances of rehabilitation had to be formally assessed and found impractical before care orders, freeing orders, residence orders or adoption orders would be made. This created an additional incentive to promote rehabilitation as the preferred option, and could be the cause of further delay. The need to be certain that the requirements of the Human Rights Act 1998 were met had also made practitioners more aware of parents' rights, and of the possibility that they might instigate proceedings if they thought these had been overlooked:

> The Human Rights Act is not going to severely change front line social work practice; what it does lay open, of course, is the capacity at a later date for people to come back and prosecute the local authority for its decision-making. (Assistant director of children and families)

Concerns about the possible implications of the legislation could also mean that difficult decisions were not taken:

> I'm not sure that some people have a very good understanding of what it is...it comes up in court quite a lot, and people will somehow use the Human Rights Act to prevent things from being done. (Senior manager, social services)

Such decisions were further complicated by perceived conflicts of interest:

> There are difficulties with the parents' right to a family life and the child's right to life and not to be injured. (Chief clerk to family proceedings court)

The difficulty was not that social workers were placing children at home with parents who might injure them. However, proving that placements with parents were not viable was a major cause of both delay and instability, and this was detrimental to the children's well-being. The findings raise the question of at what point child welfare professionals should decide that rehabilitation is not an option and a child will need to be placed for adoption. Putting off such a decision benefits neither the child nor, in the long run, the parents.

Assessment and delay

The extensive use of time-limited assessment needs to be seen within this context in which rehabilitation was promoted as the optimal outcome, even when there were contra-indications. Case-files and information from interviews suggested that professionals were often aware that assessments were unlikely to favour return to a birth parent, even when this was given as the care plan. However they sometimes needed the assessments to provide extra proof to the birth parents themselves, to other professionals and to the courts that rehabilitation was not a viable option before they could move on to other plans. In one case, for example, a psychological assessment of parenting capacity had been undertaken during proceedings in respect of the baby's older siblings. This had found that the mother was immature and unstable, and the prognosis for change was limited. The baby became looked after at birth, but the chances of rehabilitation had to be reassessed before other plans could be made. In this case, a residential assessment was undertaken, at the court's suggestion, and rapidly broke down. The child was subsequently placed for adoption.

In some cases, such as the above, the delay caused by arranging a further assessment of parenting capacity for a new baby may be regarded as a necessary factor in ensuring that the parents' rights are properly taken into account before plans for adoption are made. However, in other circumstances, better information systems might have made it easier to reach the decision that rehabilitation would be unlikely to be achievable within a timescale appropriate for a small child. In Chapter 2 we saw that drug or alcohol abuse, domestic violence or mental health problems had inhibited the parenting capacity of 24 birth mothers to the extent that their children had been looked after for at least a year. Within the timeframe of our study only two of these children were permanently reunited with their birth mothers – one a case where the father's violence had been the major issue and he had eventually left the home, and the other the child of a mother with postnatal depression who returned to both parents. None of the 11 children of drug or alcohol abusing mothers returned to them. The reason for this is not necessarily that they could not return, but that it was not safe for them to do so until their parents had overcome their difficulties. Effective adult services could evidently not be provided within a timescale that was appropriate for a child. Moreover, none of the babies went into drug or alcohol rehabilitation units with their mothers, although in one case funding was agreed for this, but the mother left the area shortly before the placement was due to begin. Instead, treatment tended to entail separation, and the babies were placed in foster care pending the mother's recovery. As one social work manager said:

> Who was paying for it, how many chances were given?... The drug and alcohol team would argue that most people going into drug rehab fail, at least for the first go. That's fine if you're dealing with adults, but if you've got a child...at a critical stage of development, as [child] was, you can't always afford to go the whole hog of two failures...when you're talking about babies and toddlers, can you ask a child to wait two years while their parent gets it together? (Social work manager)

This manager also suggested that children's services and drug and alcohol teams hold different perspectives that reflect the different client groups requiring support. Similar difficulties can be encountered when parents need to tackle alcohol addiction. Parents with drug and alcohol problems will require a huge amount of support – from both children's and adult services – if rehabilitation is to be achieved. Indeed, in Chapter 2 we saw that the most common outcome for the children of alcohol and drug misusing parents was adoption. Information systems that help professionals identify the likelihood of addressing parents' problems within a realistic timescale would both provide an incentive to improve the coordination of adult and children's services and also allow for more realistic care planning. Currently the organisation of social work around specific client groups means services are fragmented (Cleaver *et al.* 1999; Kearney, Levin and Rosen 2000; Tunnard 2002; Weir and Douglas 1999). Kroll and Taylor (2003) suggest that 'It is only through a better understanding of motivation, dependence, management or abstention and relapse that real engagement with the problems can be achieved and a longer-term resolution found' (p.299).

Relative placements

The Children Act 1989 requires any local authorities looking after a child to 'make arrangements to enable him to live with…a relative, friend or other person connected with him, unless that would not be reasonably practicable or consistent with his welfare' (Section 23:6b). Professionals were aware that adoption panels and the courts had clear expectations that placements with relatives should be considered. These placements would offer protection for the child while allowing established relationships with family members and birth parents to be maintained; contact that is often lost if children are adopted. However, family placement workers suggested that, as with birth parents, in some cases assessments of other family members were carried out even when social workers anticipated they would not be favourable.

> It's something the adoption panel will always ask about, and the courts… [Social] workers perhaps sometimes feel they almost have to do an assessment [even] where they're pretty sure the outcome's going to be negative. (Family placement worker)

> You get extended family…weighing in at a late stage in the process… right we're going to have to assess them…that quickly falls on its face…but thinking of the court time…suddenly that can create four to six months delay in the child's planning. (Family placement worker)

Even when such assessments were favourable, it was evident that placements could be jeopardised or permanence delayed because of tensions within and between family members. In one case, for example, relatives wanted to support the birth mother who was suffering from mental health difficulties; they did not feel able to commit long term to the child because they felt this implied that the mother would never be able to cope. In addition, their own circumstances and the behavioural difficulties of the child's older brother meant that the placement broke down. Only later, when it was clear that the child's mother would not be able to resume care, did the children return to these relatives.

> The whole case was…emotive…how the family tried to rally around…and keep the children within the family… Because of their own difficulties at certain points, it meant the children got moved around a bit within that… But eventually [they were able to provide] a stable home environment. (Social worker)

Contingency planning, twin tracking or concurrent planning

As is evident, at the time the 42 babies were first looked after (1996–1997) local authorities were routinely making use of *contingency planning*, whereby 'a plan is being moved forward but…a fall-back plan has been thought about and decided upon should the first plan fail' (Lowe and Murch 2002, p.8). However where, as in many of these cases, there was a strong probability that the first plan (rehabilitation to birth parents) would fail, one could argue that this introduced unnecessary delays. Given the low fulfilment rate of initial care plans, it may be desirable to make greater use of either twin tracking or concurrent planning, to minimise delay in cases where rehabilitation is unsuccessful.

Twin tracking (also known as *parallel planning*) involves:

> Working with the birth parents on rehabilitation, while the child is in a foster placement and at the same time preparing the ground for a care order or permanent placement elsewhere. (Lowe and Murch 2002, p.8)

This was not commonly used in 1996–1997; however interviews with social workers and others, held in 2001–2002, indicated that by then twin tracking was more widespread. Nevertheless, it should be acknowledged that this approach can be viewed as undermining the partnership principle, as parents are unlikely to trust professionals who say they are attempting rehabilitation home while also preparing adoption plans.

In *concurrent planning*:

> The capacity of the birth parents or wider birth family to parent the child are investigated. At the same time the child is placed with foster carers who, if the birth family cannot parent, become the adopters. (Monck *et al.* 2003, p.42)

Concurrent planning aims to minimise delay and prevent placement moves that can be damaging to child development (Katz 1990). The approach originated in Seattle, USA and has been evaluated in England with a sample of 24 children from three adoption agencies that have adopted concurrent planning and a control group of 44 children from two adoption services (Monck *et al.* 2003, p.29). Concurrent planning was found to work well for the children in Monck's study. They moved faster to permanence and experienced fewer changes of placement. Moreover, they 'did not show any evidence of harm on developmental and relationship measures' (Monck *et al.* 2003, p.269).

However, the interviews undertaken in 2001–2002 in the course of our study revealed that there was confusion among social workers about the differences between contingency planning, twin tracking and concurrent planning. It was not uncommon for social workers to say that they used concurrent planning when in fact they were describing the use of contingency planning. One of the professionals acknowledged the confusion:

> In terms of concurrent planning, I know what it is, but I'm not quite sure how it works out sometimes…it has a meaning and it doesn't have any meaning at all…it's almost as though, okay, plan A fails, plan B kicks into operation, it doesn't. You know you're talking three months, four months before…so to me, it means nothing and everything. (Social worker)

Lowe and Murch (2002, p.117) also identified variations in social workers' awareness and understanding of policies in this area. Overall, the general confusion surrounding planning highlights the need for additional social work training that not only outlines different methods of permanence planning, but also the rationale behind their use.

Decision-making and delays in achieving permanence

While policies, planning and assessments all have a bearing on the time taken to achieve permanence, there are other, additional factors. As the two detailed case studies at the end of this chapter show, children's life pathways were influenced by decisions made by parents, carers, social workers and the courts. Such decisions often arose from conflicting perspectives as to where the children's best interests genuinely lay. They were often finely balanced, with decision-makers having to weigh up a range of probable advantages and disadvantages for the children concerned, sometimes with insufficient knowledge and understanding of the relevant issues. The more complex the conflicting demands, the more likely the risk of further delay before the children achieved permanence.

Birth parents

The birth parents of children who became looked after felt they had little say in what was going to happen to them and little choice but to comply with social workers' plans, whether they agreed or not. A young mother whose baby was adopted said:

> Basically they didn't give me the choice. They wanted him to be placed into care, so I never had a choice. (Birth mother)

This particular woman later had another child whom she kept, and felt that she was offered much more support with him than with the one who was adopted. She also felt that, had the same level of support been available with her first child, she might have been able to parent him effectively as well.

The lack of choice and feelings of being ignored were, at least partly, the result of a power imbalance. Despite the acknowledged principle of working in partnership, parents' perceptions of social workers were coloured by the knowledge that they had the power to remove children, if they had not already done so. Both parties acknowledged this imbalance in the relationship:

> [The] partnership principle is laudable, although in practice it's unrealistic…because of the power relationships. (Social worker)

> Well I had to [agree with the social services plan], I had no option really. To me it's a case of agree or they'll just stop you having your child. (Birth mother)

This particular mother was eventually reunited with her child and the care order was rescinded. Nevertheless she also felt the absence of choice. With such power on one side, and powerlessness on the other, it is not surprising that birth mothers felt threatened. They felt they were constantly being observed, judged and found wanting:

> There [assessment centre], at night time, you have to give them your baby monitors, and to me…I can understand it in a way, because it's a mother and baby unit and they don't know what you're going to do, but I think in a way, you go to bed to sleep, and they're, like, listening in to you. Loss of privacy, you know. (Birth mother)

The power imbalance became more pronounced during meetings, case conferences, in court and so on, because of the inaccessibility of the language:

> [They] use all these big words, I don't bloody understand them! And they never, like, break them down for you to understand them. (Birth mother)

Their perceptions of their own powerlessness might help explain why birth mothers sometimes objected to placements with foster carers and requested that their children be moved (see Chapter 3). This could be one way that they felt able to exercise an element of control, but could also lead to disruption for the child and add to other delaying factors.

Another area where parents could exercise control was in contesting adoptions. Although they may have *felt* relatively powerless, this was one area where their actions could substantially slow down the process. In 14 cases birth parents made statements of witness against the council's plans for adoption, and/or engaged a solicitor to act on their behalf; in two cases parents successfully contested freeing orders.

Some social workers and children's guardians also raised the point that parents' solicitors could slow down the legal process by raising objections and requesting additional expert reports. However, most felt that they anticipated such objections and that these did not generally lead to delay. In many cases parents withdrew their objections or had them dismissed by the court. One should also acknowledge that the process of coming to terms with the loss of a child is a lengthy and painful business; while delays of this nature may be damaging for children, they may be necessary for parents who need to feel that they have made every effort to preserve the relationship before they can begin to let go (Department of Health 1999c).

Court issues

Any intervention by the state into the private life of families has potentially long-term and far-reaching consequences. This is particularly true where the state assumes some or all parental rights; proceedings such as committal to care or adoption therefore need to be carefully regulated. However, statutory requirements introduce processes which can themselves become significant causes of delay. In England and Wales, almost all children placed for adoption outside their extended families have already been through care proceedings. Unless the parent agrees with the plan, a freeing order is also required before an adoption order can be made. Full care orders were granted for 32 of the babies in our study; freeing orders were also granted for the 23 who were later adopted.

Care orders and freeing orders

The duration of care proceedings and the wait for court decisions can also cause delay. As noted earlier in this chapter, the length of proceedings for children in this study, from entry to care or accommodation to the granting of a full care order, took between 2 and 22 months.

Policies relating to freeing children for adoption varied considerably between local authorities. Some preferred to apply for a freeing order at the same time as a care order, while others left the freeing orders for a later date. Lowe and Murch (2002) also found a wide variation in the use of freeing orders. Different perspectives on the appropriate moment in the process to free a child led to delay for some of the babies (see Matt's case, for example, below). One of the local authority solicitors summarised the difficulties:

> We have parents' and guardians' advocates suggesting that, 'Well, it's too far in the future and it's too hypothetical, we won't give you a freeing order now'. But at the same time our adoption and fostering specialists are saying, but if we don't have a freeing order we can't compete in the market to advertise for adopters when we haven't got legal security for the child. (Local authority solicitor)

Generally there was reluctance to place children with prospective adoptive carers without the protection of a freeing order. However, the longer the babies waited the more likely they were to experience additional placement changes and/or changes of primary carer. Furthermore, the longer they waited the older, and therefore more difficult to place, they became.

Court timetables

There were differences in perspective about whether transferring cases from magistrates to county court caused delay. In one authority, the view was that delays were minimised by:

> Identifying at an early stage, if we feel it needs to go to county court, either because of the number of experts we anticipate calling, or because it's particularly difficult parents. (Local authority solicitor)

However, in another local authority, the policy to transfer cases between courts appeared to be a cause of delay and a source of frustration:

> There's been judicial authorities saying three days maximum for magistrates. If it's getting longer send it to a judge...even the average neglect case can easily take more than three days...you get cases that could competently be dealt with by a magistrate...being sent to a judge, and then that clogs up the county court. (Local authority solicitor)

Certainly there was evidence that, at county court level, lack of court time could delay proceedings. As one team leader said:

> You never get through in thirteen weeks, thirteen months is more common...which is detrimental... I've got one case...we were all ready to go in May, we've had to wait till September...that's not in anybody's

interests... The system is overloaded. But that militates against the work we're doing... (Social work manager)

Substantial further delays may also be experienced in some cases:

The issue of floating judges exacerbates that...you ask for a date...they say they can't give you a fixed judge...we'll make it a floating fixture... You take your chance [when the date comes up], that they'll have listed three cases before the same judge in the hope, on the average odds, that two will settle and one will fight. But if they've found that you've got one settled and two fighting, then one of you gives way... Then you've lost eight months, or seven months, and you start the process all over again. (Local authority solicitor)

Interviews with professionals clearly indicated that a shortage of judges and court time continues to cause delay in current cases. As Chapter 5 shows, however, new initiatives intended to reduce delays in court proceedings have been introduced since this study was undertaken.

Expert reports

The low status of social workers, and a lack of confidence in their professional expertise, meant that their assessments were frequently considered to be unreliable and further 'expert' reports were requested. This corroborates the findings of the Lord Chancellor's Department's scoping study of delay in Children Act cases (Lord Chancellor's Department 2002a). All of the social workers interviewed held either CQSW or DipSW qualifications and most had received additional post-qualifying training either in-house or externally in areas such as child protection, child development and court issues. Senior social workers and managers were also likely to have had several years of experience and additional training. They were also available to provide assistance and advice to less experienced practitioners. Children's guardians had also trained and worked as social workers, often having extensive experience in child protection and adoption work prior to taking up their current posts. Thus, while there may be a perceived lack of expertise, most of the field social workers had limited experience rather than limited knowledge, and had senior staff who were able to advise them.

Generally children's guardians were satisfied with the reports produced by social workers. Indeed, one guardian said that, if social workers were afforded more respect and remuneration, there would be less need for guardians and certainly much less need for expert reports. However, sometimes guardians requested expert reports because they felt the social worker's report to be inadequate or the assessment to be poor. In other situations a fundamental disagreement led to a request for an expert report, for example where social workers recommended rehabilitation and the guardian disagreed, or vice versa.

The courts, solicitors, and the local authority also sometimes requested expert reports in addition to those provided by social workers and children's guardians. Such requests could cause delay, as there was a shortage of psychologists and psychiatrists to do them. Moreover, in certain interviews with children's guardians, team leaders and local authority solicitors, concern was also expressed that these assessments did no more than provide information that was already known:

> Too readily lawyers suggest, 'Let's get an expert'…when you want one for a genuine reason, they've got a nine month waiting list… [Judges] are trying to use them in appropriate cases but not in the more run of the mill cases where the court should be able to depend upon a combination of the guardian and the social worker to give a view. (Local authority solicitor)

> I would say pretty much every case now, parents' solicitors will often insist on an expert. The quality of expert reports, by and large, recently has been poor. I don't think they offer…very much understanding of the case. (Local authority solicitor)

Not only was the appointment of an expert witness viewed as a waste of court time, but also as 'diminishing of social workers' competence' and costly, particularly when thorough social work assessments had already been conducted. It was also clear from interviews with social workers that when they had spent time assessing a family, meeting the parent(s), child, grandparents and significant others, they felt undermined if an additional 'expert' report was requested.

The Lord Chancellor's Department scoping study (2002a) considered that these two issues – not having the right judges available at the right time and the lack of experts – were major causes of delay in Children Act cases. This study also commented on the undervaluing of social work expertise and the shortage of experienced staff:

> Social services staff in a number of local authorities said that they were using experts to undertake part of the assessment process which would normally fall to them because of a shortage of staff with the necessary experience and expertise. While this may be an entirely proper use of experts, more worrying was the indication that some social services departments and children's guardians felt the need to instruct additional expert evidence to give their case more authority, that in effect their judgement would not be accepted without it. (Lord Chancellor's Department 2002a, p.15)

It is clear that some of the babies and very young children in our study waited too long for court decisions that were vital to secure their long-term future. As one professional pointed out:

> If in the course of court proceedings we lose time, for whatever reason, unavailability of experts, guardians not yet allocated, we are losing part of a child's childhood that we can't give back. If the case takes a year longer than it should for a combination of reasons…we've lost [part] of a kid's childhood, that we can't give them back. (Chief clerk, family proceedings court)

It is difficult to separate the various factors that contribute to delay, but it is evident that when professionals, such as social workers, guardians, judges and solicitors have competing views and expectations, then this will almost invariably have an impact on children achieving permanence. Add to this the strong possibility that parents will contest applications for orders, the problems experienced in finding suitable placements for children that will meet all or most of their needs, court directions for additional assessment, shortages of expert witnesses, and a shortage of judges and court time and it is no surprise that the process can sometimes take longer than anyone involved would wish.

One further, noteworthy factor is that the babies' experiences demonstrate an intricate relationship between delay and instability. The longer they remained looked after before permanence had been achieved, the more likely they were to experience further changes. This chapter ends with two contrasting case studies, one a fairly simple placement and return to birth parents, the other a more complex adoption. They both demonstrate the difficult decisions that have to be made in these cases, and show the complicated relationship between delay and instability which impacts on children's life pathways.

Return to birth parents

Natasha (see also Chapter 1)

Age at entry to care: 3 months
Age permanently placed: 8 months
Age ceased to be looked after: 2 years 2 months

Prior to entry to care, Natasha lived with her mother and father. She was primarily cared for by her mother, who was suffering from postnatal depression and was struggling to bond with her. Eventually her father gave up work to look after her.

Natasha became looked after at age three months, following admission to hospital with a non-accidental injury. She remained in hospital for one month, before being accommodated by the local authority under Section 20 of the Children Act 1989. Her parents visited her daily. Natasha's first foster placement was terminated after one month and she was moved to another one. This placement continued for four months, during which time an interim care order was granted. Natasha then returned to the care of her parents. Natasha remained in their care for the next year and a half, under the protection of a care order, which was then discharged.

DECISION-MAKING IN NATASHA'S CASE

The reason for social services involvement with Natasha's family stemmed from the non-accidental injury she suffered while in her parents' care.

Concerns centred on the serious injury the child sustained, both parents' refusal to admit responsibility, her mother's postnatal depression and difficulties forming an attachment to the child, and her father's drug use.

Natasha was placed with two sets of foster carers while she was looked after. The reasons for terminating the first placement after one month were threefold. First, her mother was unhappy with the care Natasha was receiving in this foster home. Second, Natasha's foster carers were going on holiday, which meant assessed contact, arranged on a daily basis, would cease for a fortnight if she went with them. Third, daily contact was problematic because of the different routines of Natasha and other foster children in the placement. Natasha remained with her second set of foster carers for four months, until she returned to the care of her parents.

Before Natasha returned home, social services carried out a comprehensive assessment of her mother and father's parenting capacity. In contact, the parents were observed to care appropriately for Natasha and they cooperated fully with social services. It was felt that support could be provided to reduce stress factors that may have contributed to Natasha's injury. Following a positive assessment Natasha returned to her parents' care. Family centre support continued and the situation was closely monitored. In addition, her father enrolled on a drug rehabilitation and reduction programme and both parents received ongoing support from their own parents, Natasha's grandparents.

Professionals involved in the case were aware that the general local authority policy on rehabilitation following non-accidental injury at this time was that:

> Rehabilitation is out of the question unless someone owns up to responsibility for an injury…[in this case] the major reasons for contemplating a return home were that we acknowledged that it would be very difficult for anybody in such circumstances to own up to responsibility… There were lots of qualities in their general care of [Natasha], as evidenced in contact, and support of extended family members, which hadn't previously been there. (Social worker)

Furthermore, a thorough assessment had been undertaken and in this case 'there was fairly good knowledge of what the stress factors were, and they were being addressed and responded to'.

In Natasha's case, three causes of delay were identified. First, there was a slight delay in obtaining a psychological assessment on her father. The report was only available four months after the court had directed it, and then it was not considered to provide any additional insight into the relevant issues. The second delay was described as purposive. It was felt that an application for the discharge of the care order should not be made until family centre support had been reduced, and the impact this had on Natasha's care had been assessed. A review was therefore convened after three months. The final delay was due to a court adjournment, meaning Natasha remained looked after for an additional two months, although by then she had already been permanently placed with her parents for 16 months (see Figure 4.2).

Adoption pathway

Matt (see also Chapter 1)

Age at entry: 7 months
Age permanence achieved: 3 years 7 months
Age adopted: 5 years

Matt's mother used drugs throughout her pregnancy and he was born with drug withdrawal symptoms. Before he became looked after he experienced two changes of address and was cared for by a number of friends and relatives although his mother was his primary carer. Throughout this time Matt remained with his two sisters, Natalie and Hannah, who were respectively three and two years older than him. All three were full siblings of dual heritage.

Matt entered local authority care at seven months of age when his mother took him to hospital with breathing difficulties and the doctor there recognised that she was under the influence of drugs. Social services had also identified a number of concerns regarding his mother's inconsistent caregiving, chaotic lifestyle and her tendency to leave Matt, Natalie

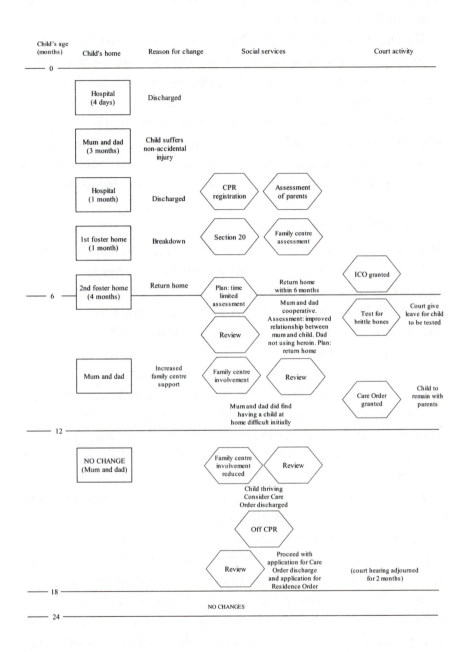

Figure 4.2: Timeline of Natasha's case

and Hannah in the care of inappropriate babysitters. An Emergency Protection Order was granted.

During the first year that the children were looked after, they experienced three changes of foster placement. Matt was separated from his sisters in his third placement; up to this point Natalie and Hannah had represented the only constant figures in his life. The siblings were reunited in their fourth foster placement. Matt remained there for two and a half years; he was then separated from his sisters and moved to a prospective adoptive home while they remained with the foster carers. Matt was adopted when he was five years old. Contact with his sisters was expected to continue.

DECISION-MAKING IN MATT'S CASE

Information from the case-file and interviews with professionals involved in Matt's case reveal a number of placement changes and causes of delay in permanent placement. In the first six months Matt was looked after he experienced three changes of placement and four primary carers. The first move can be attributed to the decision that Matt, Natalie and Hannah should change placement because the foster mother was pregnant. The second and third placement decisions were resource-led. The second placement was only available on a short-term basis, and although the third one was intended to be longer term, Matt's mother objected to the children being separated. This resulted in another move, although it did mean that Matt was (temporarily) reunited with his sisters, with whom he had lived from birth.

At admission, the care plan for these three children was adoption. However ten months then passed before a search for a match began, by which time Matt was 17 months old and his sisters aged five years two months and three years eleven months. The ideal placement was initially viewed as a dual heritage placement for all three siblings together. However, there were concerns that this would not be feasible because of difficulties in finding dual heritage adoptive placements, the number and ages of the siblings and their individual needs. Social services staff said:

> I think there might have been a hope that we could get all three adopted,
> I think that was just not do-able...do you split off the youngest one to go

off and get adopted…or do you keep all three sloshing around the care system? (Team leader)

The sisters had remained at home and experienced a lot of abuse and neglect…there was ongoing discussion about whether these siblings should be placed for adoption at all…[Matt had been] removed from home at a much earlier age, adoption was clearly achievable for him. (Social worker)

In contrast to these professional opinions, their mother's view was that Matt, Natalie and Hannah should remain together and that this objective should take precedence over finding a racially matched placement. The judge shared this view and refused to grant a freeing order when the matter first went to court on the grounds that insufficient attempts had been made to find a prospective adoptive placement for the sibling group. A racially matched placement was identified for Matt; however no appropriate placements were identified for Natalie and Hannah. The matter returned to court six months later when a freeing order was granted for Matt. Applications to free Natalie and Hannah were withdrawn, and care plans changed to long-term foster care. Unusually, the court also directed that a psychological assessment of the strength of sibling relationships should take place and the findings should be reported back to court during adoption order proceedings. In this case, the assessment led to delay in the adoption order application (see Figure 4.3). Social work professionals had reservations about the court decisions:

The primary decision-making agent in that case was the court, not us. We were overturned. (Social worker)

Points for practice

The findings discussed in this chapter raise further points that could lead to better evidence-based practice. While some of these are particularly relevant to the work of field social workers, their managers and family placement teams, others indicate changes that could be made to court practices.

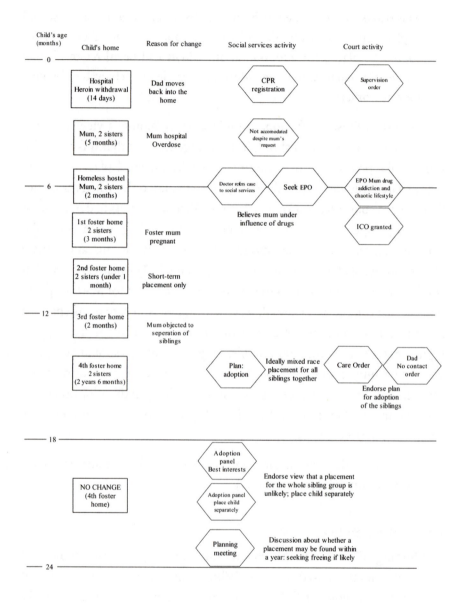

Figure 4.3: Timeline of Matt's case

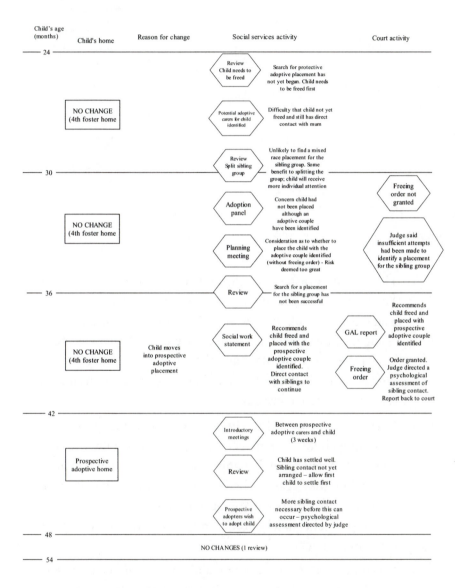

Continued on next page

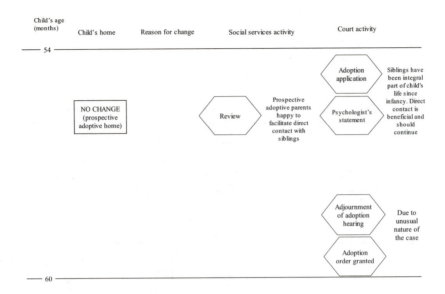

Figure 4.3 cont.

- There is an intricate relationship between delay and instability. The longer very young children wait for key decisions to be made, the more likely they are to experience additional changes of placement and/or primary carer. Moreover the longer they wait the older and therefore more difficult to place they become. Putting off a decision is a decision in itself, and can have adverse consequences.

- Delay is not necessarily in itself a negative factor. While delays in finding children permanent homes may generally be regarded as detrimental, many children achieve permanence well before they cease to be looked after. Purposive delays in revoking care orders may be beneficial in ensuring that children are adequately protected before social services cease their involvement.

- When the *mother* is very young and has herself been looked after by the local authority, it is particularly difficult to keep the best interests of the *child* at the heart of decision-making.

Practitioners may need additional support in ensuring that the child's needs are met.

- While rehabilitation may be the optimal outcome for most children, there are a small group for whom this is not the case; practitioners may need support in identifying these children at an early stage and in making realistic care plans for them.

- Concurrent planning may increase stability and reduce delays in achieving permanence for very young children. However there is much confusion concerning different kinds of permanence planning, and practitioners are likely to need additional training to clarify the issues and help them understand the rationale behind the various approaches.

- The provision of adult services, such as drug rehabilitation, often fails to take account of children's timescales. Joint planning between adults' and children's services might enable professionals to work more closely together and to consider adults' needs as *parents*. Decisions that rest on the likelihood of a parent overcoming mental health or substance abuse problems within a timescale that meets the child's needs might be informed by making better use of evidence concerning what agencies have been able to achieve in the past.

- Placements with relatives may prove very beneficial to a child, but they should not be regarded as a cheap or easy option. As with all foster carers, it is important to ensure that relatives are fully aware of the nature and extent of the commitment before a placement is made. Many relatives will also require high levels of support if they are to meet the child's needs, particularly if the placement causes tensions with the birth parents.

- Parents who feel disempowered are more likely to contest care orders and freeing orders, and introduce further delays into the process of finding permanent placements for their children. Helping parents feel that their views have been listened to and acknowledged may improve stability and reduce delays.

- Court procedures also contribute to delays in children achieving permanence. Such delays could be reduced by: better timing of applications for freeing orders; more active case management; addressing shortages of court time; and more considered use of expert reports.

Note

1   These regulations applied at the time the study was undertaken and are still largely in place, although some will be superseded following the implementation of the Adoption and Children Act 2002.

Chapter 5

Key Findings, Conclusions and Implications for Policy, Practice and Training

Introduction

In this book we set out to answer a number of questions about very young children who remain in care or accommodation for a long time. We sought to find out why a high proportion of a long-stay group of children looked after by local authorities in England were babies, admitted before their first birthday; why they remained so long in care; and why proportionately more came from some authorities than others. We explored further the evidence of instability within the care system, seeking to discover why these very young children changed placement so frequently and why even a small number of their placements disrupted. We tried to identify which children were most likely to be successfully reunited with their families and which would need to be placed for adoption, and we looked at how their early adverse experiences had influenced their current well-being. In this final chapter we bring together some of the key findings from the study that forms the focus of this book and discuss whether changes in legislation and policy that have occurred since these children were admitted to the care of the local authorities will have addressed some of the concerns raised by their experiences. We conclude by identifying those issues which recent changes are unlikely to have resolved, and which will continue to have implications for policy, practice and the training of professionals.

Key findings

Children's and parents' circumstances

The Children Act 1989 lays on local authorities the duty to 'promote the upbringing of…children by their families' so long as this is consistent with the duty to 'safeguard and promote the well being of children within their area who are in need' (Section 17 (1) (a and b)). The children whose experiences have been discussed in this book are essentially those for whom these two principles were most likely to come into conflict. They were all very young and had all spent over half their lives in care by the time they were identified by the research team; information about their needs and experiences both within the care system and prior to entry should increase the evidence base on which social workers are able to draw in making some of their most difficult decisions: identifying those children whose parents will be able to meet their needs within an acceptable timeframe and those for whom rehabilitation is not a viable option, whose welfare can only be adequately safeguarded and promoted by permanent placement away from home.

The 42 babies we studied entered care or accommodation before they were 12 months old and had all been looked after by local authorities for at least a year. They came from vulnerable families where parents were struggling in difficult circumstances. Many of their parents were either single and unsupported or in difficult relationships, characterised by domestic violence. Parents had often had a series of relationships so that many of the children had half- or step-siblings, frequently of different ethnicity from themselves. Over half of the mothers had problems with drug and alcohol abuse, domestic violence or mental ill health; many of them had multiple problems. Those who showed no evidence of any of these difficulties nevertheless had other problems such as debt, homelessness or mild learning disabilities, or were extremely young and immature. Fourteen of the parents had themselves been looked after as children. Moreover parental problems had often affected the children: at birth a small number suffered from drug withdrawal symptoms or foetal alcohol syndrome. A greater number were later physically abused or neglected – two had sustained head injuries that left them with complex and serious health needs. All but five of the babies had been placed on the child protection register, either at birth or soon afterwards. These babies would therefore have had complex needs, often exacerbated by their early life experiences. They would have been demanding children, who would not have been easy to look after; their carers would have had to possess excellent parenting skills, and yet we know that there were many reasons why their parents would have found it difficult to develop such expertise.

Instability

Many of the babies' early adverse experiences were compounded by a lack of continuity and stability. Because they were so young, it was possible to map the changes they had experienced from birth until they were aged five or six. The study reveals extensive instability within their birth families before these children entered care or accommodation. Before their first birthdays, while living with their families, 11 of the babies had had four or more addresses, 18 had had at least two primary carers and 5 had had four or more. For some children this experience of constant change and instability continued after they entered the care of the local authorities: during the first year that they were looked after, while 14 of the babies stayed in the same placement, 17 had three or more. Only 4 children retained the same primary carer throughout the time that they were looked after, and 19 had four or more. In many cases being looked after offered little more stability – although considerably more safety – than remaining with birth parents might have done. Such constant experience of change is likely to have had a considerable and damaging impact on the ability of these very young children to form secure attachments.

It was possible to track the reasons for moves within the care system. Of the 101 moves recorded for these children, 25 were unplanned transitions. Placements with parents and relatives were the most likely to break down, either because the social workers regarded their care as unsatisfactory or because the parents themselves were finding it impossible to cope. Both the courts and social services tended to regard return to birth family as the optimal outcome, and some of these disruptions were anticipated as part of the process of demonstrating that this was not a viable permanent solution. A small number of other placements disrupted because foster carers could not cope with the exceptional demands made of them, particularly in working in partnership with hostile or demanding parents.

The majority of moves in care, however, were due not to disruptions, but to planned transitions, many of which could be regarded as positive changes. Some occurred because children were moved between foster carers and their own parents, so that parenting skills could be assessed, or reunification tried out. Other positive moves were from a temporary placement to a permanent home with long-term foster carers or an adoptive family. Moves to bring sibling groups back together or to place children from minority ethnic groups with more appropriate foster carers accounted for other transitions. However the strength of sibling relationships was rarely assessed, although attempts to place groups together were a major cause of delays in achieving permanence and, in some instances, of placement breakdown.

Not all planned transitions were likely to prove positive experiences for the children concerned. Within the context of the children's ages, and the transitory lives that so many had experienced before they became looked after, it is of some concern that a number of babies were also placed temporarily elsewhere when foster carers went on holiday. However, perhaps the most damaging experience was that of those young children who spent several months securely placed with foster carers who were then refused permission to adopt them on the grounds that they were unsuitable as permanent carers. Findings from the study suggest that there were different standards of approval for adoptive parents, foster carers and relative carers, yet the children's current needs remained constant, wherever they were placed.

There is some evidence that continuing instability both before and during their time in care or accommodation had left some of these babies with an enduring sense of insecurity. At the time they were interviewed at age five or six, a small number were displaying behaviour patterns indicative of hyperactivity and conduct disorders.

By the end of the study, five or six years after they entered care or accommodation, 23 of the children had been adopted, two had been permanently placed with relatives in their extended family and three were still looked after. Fourteen of the babies had returned to birth parents, but only one of these was a child who was permanently reunited with a mother who had had problems with drug and alcohol abuse, domestic violence or mental ill health. While none of the adoptive placements had broken down, some of the children who had returned to birth parents or relatives were no longer living with the family member with whom they had, in theory, been permanently placed.

Delays

It was obviously important that these very young children should be placed permanently as quickly as possible so that they could experience some continuity in their lives and develop secure attachments to adults who could provide them with a stable home. Yet the babies were looked after by the local authorities for an average of 31 months before they were adopted or finally restored to their birth families. Findings from the study shed further light on the reasons for delays in their achieving permanence.

First, it was evident that although these children remained the *responsibility* of the local authorities for several years, some of the delays were more apparent than actual. The average length of time before the children found a permanent home (15 months) was about half the average time they spent formally in care or accommodation. The difference between the two timeframes could be considered an administrative delay, and was not likely to affect the well-being of – or even to be noticed by – such very young children, for whom emotional and physical permanence is much more important than legal status. When children were placed with their own parents but protected by care orders there was evidence of purposive delays, where the legal status was retained until such time as their situation was considered stable. Similarly, when children were placed with adoptive families, evidence that the placement was likely to last was needed before an adoption order could be made.

Notwithstanding the above, there were other, less positive, reasons why such very young children remained looked after for lengthy periods. These children were very young and vulnerable, and it was not safe for many of them to return home until parents' problems had been addressed.

However rehabilitation to birth parents was frequently impossible within a timeframe that was compatible with the babies' developmental needs. Adult services took little account of children's needs, and so those parents who accepted treatment had to wait for it while their childen grew up away from them. Those children who did return to birth parents were either rehabilitated after an abusive partner had left the home, or eventually returned to a previously non-resident birth father. Some returned to permanent placements with other relatives, under the protection of a residence order – another procedure that lengthened the gap between permanence and ceasing to be looked after.

The prevalence of parents with drug, alcohol or mental health problems and the poor coordination of adult treatment programmes with the needs of dependent children appeared to be the main reason why there was a disproportionate number of these very young looked after children from one of the participating local authorities. The disproportionate numbers of babies from another authority may not have been a true reflection of the situation, as the numbers were very small; alternatively there was evidence that those children who were looked after by this local authority had exceptionally high and complex needs, which may have increased their length of stay.

There was only one baby who returned to a mother with drug, alcohol or mental health problems – and this child's father was living in the home. Adoption was the most likely permanent solution for these children, but this could not be easily achieved. All professionals involved were also mindful that the courts would require proof that permanent placement with parents or relatives was not viable before other arrangements could be made. However obtaining such proof was a major factor that contributed to delays in achieving permanence, particularly as twin tracking was rarely used, and concurrent planning never used.

Delays were also related to shortages of court time, objections from parents and the difficulties of obtaining expert reports. This latter issue was exacerbated by the poor status of social workers, whose judgements were frequently set aside by other professionals in favour of 'expert' opinions from psychologists and psychiatrists who had less knowledge of the case.

Lack of resources also contributed to delays. There were sometimes substantial delays in matching prospective adopters with children, particularly if they were of dual or multiple heritage or were part of a sibling group. Seven out of eighteen babies were not matched with prospective adopters within the target time frame of six months from the best interests decision.

Finally two further, significant, points emerged from these findings. First, there was an obvious relationship between movement and delay. Twelve of the thirteen babies who spent more than 18 months looked after before they found a permanent home had three or more placements; the same was true of only seven of the eighteen who achieved permanence within a year. The longer children waited for a permanent placement, the more likely they were to experience further change and instability, and the more their chances of developing secure attachments were jeopardised. It should be a matter of concern that some of these infants, who had been admitted to care before their first birthday, were becoming 'hard to place' by the time they found a permanent placement. Second, it became evident that delays had their own consequences, so that putting off a decision, or waiting to take a particular action did not mean that nothing happened. Children continued to develop and relationships changed during the interim period. In particular these very young children became attached to temporary carers, so that a move to what might have appeared a more appropriate placement became increasingly problematic. It was not always apparent to practitioners that a point would be reached where the need for stability might have to take precedence over the desirability of reuniting sibling groups, finding a same or similar race placement or, indeed, reunification with a previously absent birth parent. Moreover practitioners were not always aware that strong attachments to carers who were less than ideal were nevertheless an important factor that might eventually outweigh other considerations.

Implications of subsequent policy changes for the life pathways of babies in care

The study explored in this book is one of several that have raised concerns about the delays and instability inherent in the care system, although it is among the very few that have specifically focused on the impact of these problems on the well-being of very young children (see also Cousins *et al.* 2003; Department of Health 2000a; Ivaldi 2000). The babies entered the care of the local authorities in 1996–1997 and were traced until 2002. As Chapter 1 indicated, during that period, and subsequently, a number of policy and legislative changes were introduced, with the aim of addressing some of the issues raised by the experiences of these children and others like them. How far is their impact likely to have improved the experiences of similar children who have since entered care in England and Wales?

Improving stability

New Labour policy on Modernising Social Services (Department of Health 1998b) was launched in 1998, about a year after these babies entered care. For the first time the government set out explicitly its expectations of social services: clear, national objectives were announced, key targets were set and a comprehensive system for monitoring and managing performance was introduced (Department of Health 1998b, 7.4). The Quality Protects initiative was launched to help authorities meet these objectives by 'remedying deficits in the standards of care offered to looked after children and other children needing social services support' (Department of Health 1998b, 3.25).

Objective One was 'to ensure that children are securely attached to carers capable of providing safe and effective care for the duration of childhood' (Department of Health 1998b, 7.4). A National Priority Guidance target was set to reduce to no more than 16 per cent in all authorities, by 2001, the number of looked after children who experienced three or more placements in one year (Department of Health 1999a). Local authorities could use funding made available under the Quality Protects initiative to increase the stability of placements (Robbins 1999, 2000, 2001) and progress towards this target was monitored using the Performance Assessment Framework (Department of Health 1999b). The national figures indicate that it was met (Department for Education and Skills, 2004b). In spite of some concerns (see below), it does seem clear that measures such as this have successfully brought to the attention of both managers and practitioners the importance of ensuring that looked after children have adequate opportunities to develop secure attachments. Overall, children who enter the care system now are unlikely to experience quite the same levels of change as did the babies we studied. There is, however, still much to be done; although nationally the target was met, a third of authorities had still not achieved this relatively modest level of stability by 2003 (Department for Education and Skills 2004b, p.7). Moreover there is evidence that only a few authorities analyse the data collected for government performance indicators to identify which children move most (and least) frequently (Gatehouse and Ward 2003). The data from the wider cohort from which the 42 babies were identified suggest that the infants moved at least as frequently as the teenagers (Ward 2004). Until authorities are routinely monitoring the frequency with which very young children change placement and the reasons for such moves, issues of discontinuity and transience for this population will not be adequately addressed.

We have seen that a lack of suitable placements meant that some children were initially placed with short-term carers until more appropriate arrangements could be made, thereby engendering additional moves. This was particularly true for sibling groups of three or more, or for children of dual or mixed heritage. These issues also sometimes re-emerged when adoptive placements were being sought. This reiterates the findings of other studies, which have also emphasised how frequently placements are made in emergencies, and how these are more likely to be unsatisfactory, and to fail (see Sinclair 2005). Across the UK, there is an estimated shortage of about 10,000 foster carers, a factor which inevitably contributes to the instability of care (BAAF and the Fostering Network 2005). Attempts have been made to address these issues at a national level. Under the Choice Protects programme (2003–2006) additional funding has been made available to local authorities to expand and strengthen their fostering services and improve outcomes for looked after children by providing better placement stability, matching and choice. Extensive work is being undertaken to improve the stability of placements through increasing the range of options available and through improving the status, support and training of the workforce. The Children Act 2004 (Section 49) allows for secondary legislation to be made to introduce a minimum fostering allowance to be made available to all foster carers, including kinship carers, and work is currently under way to establish the level at which it should be set.

Delay

This book has also explored the damaging effects of delay inherent in the care system. The children waited for viable care plans to be agreed; for sufficient proof that they could or could not return permanently to their birth parents; for appropriate placements to be found; or for court processes to be completed. Each delay increased the likelihood of further instability and change, and each delay meant that the children were older and less likely to settle easily into a permanent placement by the time one was found. As we noted in Chapter 1, ours is only one of many studies that have identified delay and its consequences as a major issue to be addressed if outcomes for looked after children are to be improved (see also Department of Health 2000a; Harwin *et al.* 2001; Ivaldi 2000; Rowe and Lambert 1973). At a national level, the prevalence of delays in achieving permanence and their potential impact on children's well-being increasingly became a cause of concern during the period that the 42 babies were looked after by the authorities. Such concerns were reinforced by evidence that, although the numbers of children entering local authority care were diminishing, the average length of stay – and therefore the cost of care episodes – was increasing. At the heart of such concerns was the question of whether too many children were waiting in the care system with unrealistic plans for reunification with parents whose problems could not be addressed within an appropriate timescale, a point repeatedly raised by the findings from our study. Evidence that in some authorities prospective adoptive parents were sometimes refused approval on apparently arbitrary and unnecessary grounds – a point also supported by some of the findings from our study – lent force to the argument that a number of children were being denied the opportunity of finding permanent placements through adoption, although this might most appropriately meet their needs (Department of Health 2000a).

The White Paper *Adoption: A New Approach* (Department of Health 2000b), followed by the Adoption and Children Act 2002, have provided the policy and legislative framework by which the government plans to address these issues. This major initiative includes, among other arrangements, provision to encourage more people to come forward as prospective adoptive parents and to allow some of the restrictions on their approval to be removed or reassessed by independent reviewers; provision to facilitate the process by which foster carers can adopt children placed with them; plans to cut delays in matching children with appropriate adopters by putting the Adoption Register on a statutory footing; and arrangements to introduce a new Special Guardianship order to provide permanence for children who cannot return to their birth families but for whom adoption is inappropriate. Within this framework, local authorities have been set targets to increase by 40 per cent within five years the number of children adopted from care and to increase by 95 per cent within four years the proportion of looked after children placed with prospective adopters within 12 months of a best interests decision (Department of Health 2002). The accompanying National Adoption Standards (Department of Health 2001b) provide detailed timescales for each stage of the adoption process; annual statistical returns monitor the implementation of timescales and progress towards targets on a national basis.

Within the Adoption and Permanence initiative there are also moves to reduce delays in the court process. The professionals interviewed in the course of the study described in this book frequently described shortages of judges and children's guardians, and expert witnesses such as psychologists and psychiatrists, as well as overloaded court timetables, as continuing causes of delay, influencing the length of time children remain looked after. The chief clerk from the family proceedings court in one of the authorities indicated that there were over 50 cases waiting to be allocated to guardians. A common strand throughout interviews was the increased delay caused by cases going to county rather than magistrate's courts (see Chapter 4). Following research undertaken during the period that the children in our study were looked after by authorities (Lord Chancellor's

Department 2002a), a protocol on *Judicial Case Management in Public Law Children Act Cases* (Lord Chancellor's Department 2002b) has been issued. This came into force in 2003 and is intended to address many of the reasons for delay in court processes identified by our study. The protocol is designed to encourage inter-agency working and gives detailed guidance on the steps that ought to be taken at each stage of the process, including assessment, care plan, court application, and preparation for case conference, with timescales for their completion. It is accompanied by a national target, set by the Court Service, to complete 70 per cent of care proceedings cases within 40 weeks.

One further policy initiative introduced during the course of this study as part of the Quality Protects programme, was the implementation of the *Framework for the Assessment of Children in Need and their Families* (Department of Health, Department for Education and Employment and Home Office 2000). The emphasis is on adopting an ecological approach which explores the inter-relationship between parenting capacity, family and environmental factors and children's developmental needs; identifying the precise nature of needs and the reasons for them; assessing the potential for change in the child and the family; identifying strengths as well as weaknesses; ensuring that plans flow logically from assessments; and promoting inter-agency working. Assessment is regarded as an iterative process that continues throughout the period of intervention. The implementation of the Framework should improve the evidence base on which decisions are made and lead to better planning for children and families. Its introduction should have facilitated difficult decisions, such as those that had to be made about the young children in this study (Cleaver and Walker 2004).

The *Assessment Framework* has now been linked with the *Looking After Children* project to form the *Integrated Children's System* (ICS), which provides 'an assessment, planning, intervention and reviewing model for all children in need' and is due for implementation in 2006 (Department of Health 2000c, p.1). This new, computerised system, is designed to enable data about individual children to be used to inform planning at both individual and strategic levels. The ICS forms a key element in an ongoing initiative to improve the structure and use of information in children's services, yet another policy development that should improve the delivery of services to these very young children.

These earlier initiatives to reduce instability and delay, introduce more holistic assessments and improve the use of information in children's services have now been incorporated into the major government agenda on *Every Child Matters* (HM Government 2003). The delivery of this relatively new policy agenda is enabled by the Children Act 2004, and aims to change the way in which services are provided to children and families in order to improve their well-being, safeguard and promote their welfare, identify and protect those at risk of significant harm, and improve support for families. The primary objective is to improve outcomes for all children in England and Wales, and reduce the gap between the most vulnerable and their peers. The initiative has the potential to ensure that children such as those in this study receive a service that more closely meets their needs. Areas within the initiative that might in the future benefit very young, very vulnerable children are the emphasis on early intervention, information sharing, integrated working and workforce reform. In particular, plans to improve the status, skills and remuneration of foster carers – including kinship carers – might have addressed some of the issues faced by the children we studied.

Early impact of policy developments

As is evident from the above, performance management is now a key feature of policy implementation in England and Wales. Central government sets specific targets for the improvement of services, and requires local authorities to provide data on an extensive – and increasing – range of performance indicators selected to demonstrate progress towards their achievement. There are real concerns that performance management has increased bureaucracy at the expense of social work interactions with families; that the focus on reaching targets has deflected the attention of managers away from meeting children's needs, creating perverse incentives, for instance, to retain children in inappropriate placements rather than risk increasing the number of moves; and that too much attention is given to gathering the data required for national returns, and too little to exploring what they reveal about the experiences of individual children. Notwithstanding such concerns, the requirement to provide extensive data on performance has introduced a degree of transparency into the work of children's services that was previously lacking. For instance, local authorities now know how many looked after children attain GCSEs or remain in touch with social services after they have moved to independent living – evidence that was unavailable before 1998.

There is some evidence from the national statistics that the situation of very young, very vulnerable children such as those in this study is beginning to change. More children are being adopted from care, and best interest decisions are being made more quickly. There is also evidence of improved stability of placements for those who remain looked after. However delays in the adoption process do not yet appear to be decreasing, and instability is still unacceptably high in some authorities (Department for Education and Skills 2005b, pp.5–6).

Cohort Two

The national statistics provide only very broad indicators of trends. To complement them we also have more detailed evidence from the six local authorities that participated in our study. The babies were all part of one cohort of long looked after children, followed over a period of time. We later identified a second cohort of children, in the care of the same authorities, and selected on the same criteria as those in the first, the only difference being that they entered care or accommodation about two and a half years later (between 1 October 1998 and 30 September 1999) (see Ward *et al.* forthcoming a). Information from the second group, coupled with evidence from interviews, indicates that some progress was made between 1996 and 2002, thus addressing *some* of the causes of change and delay identified in this study.

Both cohorts of children were looked after by the authorities for between 12 and 24 months before inclusion in our study; in both, there were significantly more babies admitted to care before their first birthday than children of any other age. There was a slight downward trend in the number of placements experienced by the babies in Cohort Two, suggesting that measures being taken to improve stability could be beginning to have some impact. However this trend was not significant and might well have been due to chance. In Cohort One, 17 (41%) of babies had three or more placements in the first year they were looked after, as compared with 21 (38%) in Cohort Two.

The interviews revealed that, by 2002 when they were undertaken, parenting assessments in residential units appeared to be used less frequently than previously. These placements were utilised in a number of cases in the first cohort; it was not uncommon for them to break down, meaning the child had an additional move. Nevertheless, in 2002, foster carer shortages still meant that children were placed with whichever carers were available and that compromises had to be made. Moreover, the shortage extended to adopters:

> We could actually approve more adopters if we had more social workers in the adoption team...but unfortunately the number of looked after children needing adoption has gone beyond that, so we've been over-taken by numbers, if you like. (Social work manager)

Thus, even though local authorities had recruited additional foster carers and adopters, by 2002 there was still little placement choice, an issue which, as we have seen, current government policy is attempting to address.

Care plans and twin tracking

Table 5.1 shows the care plans at entry for the babies in the two cohorts. There were some differences here although these were not statistically reliable. While 14 (36%) of the those in Cohort One entered care with a plan to remain with or return to their birth family, this was only true of 10 (18%) in Cohort Two. We have seen that very few of these babies were in fact reunited, but that the expectation that they would be was a major cause of change and delay. More realistic planning may subsequently have been put into operation, also reflected by the increase in the proportion of babies for whom the immediate plan was adoption, from just three of the 42 (7%) in the first cohort, on whom this book has focused, to 11 out of 56 (20%) in the second. However, an alternative explanation is that the rise in the number of initial care plans for adoption relates to differences in parental profiles in Cohorts One and Two, rather than a broad-based shift in policy and practice. A higher percentage of parents in Cohort Two were found to be suffering mental ill health, drug abuse and alcohol misuse, and as we have seen, parents with these problems were least likely to be reunited with their children.

Table 5.1: Care plans at entry for children in the two cohorts (n=95)

	Cohort One	Cohort Two
Time-limited assessment	17 (44%)	29 (52%)
Remain with/return to birth family	14 (36%)	10 (18%)
Live with relatives/friends	1 (3%)	2 (4%)
Special residential placement	0	1 (2%)
Long-term placement	1 (3%)	1 (2%)
Adoption	3 (8%)	11 (20%)
Other	3 (8%)	2 (4%)
Total	39	56

The proportion of babies with a plan for time-limited assessment had risen, from 17 out of 42 (44%) in Cohort One to 29 out of 56 (52%) in Cohort Two. As we have seen in Chapters 3 and 4, information from case-files and interviews indicated that in 1996–1997 later assessments as well as failed attempts at rehabilitation could lead to additional movement and delay. Interviews with senior practitioners suggest that, by 2002, this situation might have begun to improve, particularly since, by then, greater emphasis had been placed on twin tracking rather than relying on contingency planning.

> The courts expect it…we expect social workers now…to be looking simultaneously, both rehabilitation, extended family, and possibly per-manence… In the past, they'd wait until the assessment process was

finished...then they'd decide on rehabilitation, that could be three, four months...and then they'd think about booking the adoption panel, and maybe a three, four month delay. So, it's improving. (Social work manager)

There is certainly an informal...an expectation that twin tracking...is considered at a very early stage within care proceedings, so that we avoid delay if it becomes apparent that rehabilitation is unlikely to succeed. (Local authority solicitor)

However, another respondent offered a different perspective by suggesting how parents may feel regarding twin tracking if the matter is not handled sensitively:

[In the court we have had] parents who are still disputing the care plan for a child to go for adoption and are saying 'This child ought to come back and live with us', and the local authority saying 'Please may we have leave to advertise this child, using photographs, in the adoption quarterly magazines.' ...You can imagine the horror that comes from this side of the court, from the parents, saying 'We haven't even decided'. (Chief clerk, family proceedings court)

Overall, it would appear that babies entering the system more recently than 1996–1997 might fare slightly better in terms of a reduced number of placements, fewer residential assessments and more widespread use of twin tracking. Delays in the court process are also now being better acknowledged and addressed. Nevertheless, many of the other issues that led to change and delay remain problematic and are unlikely to be easily resolved. They reflect the difficulty of making complex decisions that will have a lasting impact on the lives and well being of very vulnerable families. We conclude by discussing how far the findings from the study convey messages for changes to practice and training that might facilitate such decisions.

Further messages for training and practice

While both national and local statistical information indicates that progress was being made during the course of the study, there were nevertheless numerous indicators from case-files and interviews of areas where practice might be improved. In particular, there is still an evident need for practitioners to improve their ability to build on the evidence from assessments and to articulate the strengths and weaknesses of factors within the domains of 'parenting capacity' and 'family and environment' in order to evaluate how they impact on children's development. Such analyses would then provide the rationale for making plans and identifying appropriate interventions. They would also offer a baseline against which subsequent progress can be monitored.

There is, for instance, evidence that, in spite of an explicit sequence of processes for constructing and reviewing plans in complex social work cases, supported by detailed regulations (Department for Education and Skills 2003), care plans are not always carefully thought through, but are still frequently made and changed in reaction to circumstances:

> I don't think I could easily locate a decision making forum where we sat down with the evidence as it was then, and said what would happen…it is very hard to give voice to how frenetic, chaotic, shambolic sometimes working in a social services office can be. And really, it's a case of momentum being built up, building up to this alternative course of action, and it's just inevitable, it just kind of flows on inevitably. I don't think there was any crisp punctuation of our activity, to say 'Okay, let's take stock. Where are we going now?' (Social worker)

Other recent studies have also shown that, while a wealth of information is now gathered in the course of social work interactions, and much of this is now standardised and structured, too little attention is spent on analysing its implications and developing plans that address identified needs (Cleaver and Walker 2004; Cleaver *et al.* forthcoming). Moreover it is evident that, in spite of greatly increased requirements to provide data for government returns, much more use could be made of such information to support both practitioners and managers in providing a service that delivers better outcomes for children and families (Gatehouse, Statham and Ward 2004).

This book produces a wealth of evidence that could be used to help professionals move towards more proactive planning. Knowing that a child has been passed repeatedly from one member of the family to another *before* becoming looked after could be used as evidence that rehabilitation to a stable home with relatives is unlikely. A number of children were placed at birth because a sibling had been abused. In these circumstances parenting capacity had to be reassessed because:

> You cannot judge the parent on previous assessments, *unless* (emphasis added) there is an acknowledgement that nothing appears to have changed. (Chief clerk to the family proceedings court)

These very young children were placed with foster carers pending such assessments, and then sometimes moved to parents and back to carers again while parenting capacity was being evaluated. Yet proactive planning would have meant that evidence of improved parenting capacity might have been gathered during the pregnancy, or an assessment arranged to take place immediately following the child's birth.

Not all the authorities had information systems that allowed practitioners and managers to make use of data about past capacity in informing their current decisions, yet again this would have been of considerable value. Knowing, for instance, that practically no very young children of drug abusing parents had been able to return home once they had been looked after for a year would have made it easier to decide to move towards adoption. Such information would also have provided an incentive to negotiate better coordination with adult services. Knowing how rare it was for birth fathers who had not previously lived with their children to be able to provide a long-term stable home after a long care episode would have informed decisions about permanency plans, and provided a strong argument for offering extensive and continuing support when such placements were made. Knowing how few permanent placements had been found for sibling groups of three or more in the recent past, and how long some children had waited for the unattainable, would have made it easier to decide when other groups might need to be split. Such evidence might also have led to a recruitment drive to find more foster or adoptive families with this capacity. Increased availability of data on past performance, such as those given in these examples, might also eventually mean that plans which ignored such evidence would need to justify why a particular case was likely to be an exception to the rule. The implementation of the Integrated Children's System, designed as an electronic case recording system with a direct link to the authority's database, should mean that such information can be more easily retrieved and be made more readily available to practitioners (Gatehouse *et al.* 2004). Improvements in the availability and functionality of technology, supported by substantial government funding (Department for Education and Skills 2005c), might mean that in the not too distant future this expectation becomes a reality.

This book also raises questions about the nature of partnership. One of the principles of the Children Act 1989 is that: 'the development of a working partnership with parents is usually the most effective route to providing supplementary or substitute care for children' (Department of Health 1990, p.8). Kufeldt, Armstrong and Dorosh (1995) found that parents' acceptance of a placement facilitates partnership working with social workers and foster carers. Yet there is an obvious imbalance of power in this relationship. In the study discussed in this book, some parents found themselves to be very unequal partners and expressed their frustration through actions that caused further delay, disruption and instability for their children. Better skills in communicating with parents and greater transparency in the authority's expectations both of how they can demonstrate their capacity to change and of their continuing relationship with their children, might lead to closer partnerships and less disruption.

There was also evidence about the mixed messages that foster carers receive from social services. The role of local authority foster carers has changed considerably over the last ten years or so, and they are now required to work much more closely with the child's birth family. Some of them felt unsupported in this capacity, and a few placements broke down because foster carers found that parents were too hostile, or contact arrangements placed too many demands on them (see also Sinclair *et al.* 2004). Their role must be confusing at times, for they are both expected to support birth parents and to look after very young children who may be placed with them for months or even years. It must be difficult for them to know how far they should allow themselves to form attachments, and this may be one of the reasons for the rather impersonal care given to some of the older children in the original study (see Skuse and Ward 2003). The quality of care was not raised as a specific issue with this smaller group of very young children. However some of the babies' foster carers were regarded as suitable long-term carers, while still not providing a high enough standard of care to be regarded as potential adopters. Evidence of different standards of approval for relative carers, foster carers and adopters, all of whom are expected to meet the complex needs of very vulnerable children, would merit further exploration.

There were additional issues for relative carers, who sometimes found they had taken on a much more complicated and onerous task than they had originally anticipated. The findings from this study reinforce one of the messages for managers and practitioners from another study undertaken by one of the authors: placements with relatives require adequate resources and high levels of support if they are to succeed – they are not a cheap and easy option (Ward *et al.* 2004).

Implications for social work training

Finally, this book has many messages for social work training. There are numerous indications as to where the knowledge base needs to be strengthened in order to provide better evidence-based practice. The experiences of the babies we studied demonstrate again and again the importance of social workers and other professionals in such cases having a ready understanding of child development and, in particular, theories of attachment. Such an understanding is necessary to appreciate the potentially adverse, long-term consequences of extensive experiences of instability in early life; it should inform decisions about placing children away from home, and moving them from one carer to another. Such an understanding is also necessary if practitioners are to develop the skills they need to assess the strength of children's attachments to birth parents and carers and to identify indicators of concern.

Attachment theory is also important in understanding children's relationships with siblings, some of whom may have taken on a parental role when birth parents were labouring with problems such as mental ill health, drug or alcohol addiction (Aldridge and Becker 2003). However an important message from this study is that practitioners need to develop a better understanding of the complexity of sibling relationships in some of the families with whom they work. These fell into many different patterns, as families had separated and been reconstituted. The over-riding assumption was always that siblings should be placed together, yet there may well have been instances in which extreme jealousy or parental scapegoating might have rendered separation more appropriate. There were, however, only two cases in which the strength of these relationships was formally assessed. Improved understanding of the nature and strength of sibling relationships in different family contexts would improve the evidence base on which such difficult decisions are made.

The babies' experiences also demonstrate that social workers need to develop a thorough understanding of issues such as parental drug and alcohol abuse, mental health problems and domestic violence and their potential impact on very young children. Decision-making would be better informed if practitioners were more aware, for instance, that drug abuse in pregnancy produces far more serious long-term implications for the children concerned than withdrawal symptoms at birth (Moe 2002; Slinning 2003); or if evidence of the length of time it takes for parents to overcome drug and alcohol addiction, and the long-term effectiveness of rehabilitation programmes was more widely disseminated. As other studies have demonstrated, improved understanding of mental health problems, and the risk and protective factors for young children whose parents have such difficulties would also lead to more effective decision-making (Cleaver *et al.* 1999; Falkov 2002).

Findings from this study also have implications for the development of social work skills. Poor planning meant that much social work decision-making was reactive rather than proactive, resulting in sudden and unexpected changes of circumstances for the children: this is yet another study that demonstrates the need for better training on the preparation and purpose of care plans and on communication with service users. The findings demonstrate that practitioners were confused about the differences between contingency planning, twin tracking and concurrent planning (see also Lowe and Murch 2002; Monck *et al.* 2003). An exploration of these concepts, together with an evaluation of their implications for both children, foster carers and birth families, might form an integral part of such training. It could also cover how parents might be more involved in the planning process and brought into discussions of those issues which will have to be addressed if their children's needs are to be adequately met.

The implementation of the Integrated Children's System (ICS) will have considerable implications for the development of social work training in many areas that are relevant to the findings from our study on very young children in care. Much of the information recorded on social work case files was hard to find, and some of it was out of date. There were a number of significant inaccuracies. If the ICS is to be effectively implemented, practitioners will need to develop a better understanding of the need for accurate and timely recording. They will also need training in basic IT skills to manage the system, although the evidence suggests that there have been substantial advances in this area, at least in the pilot authorities (Cleaver *et al*. forthcoming). However, if practitioners and managers are to make full use of the database, so that past evidence informs future decision-making in complex cases such as those of the young children we studied, they will need to become more skilled in the analysis of data. A greater understanding of probability theory would be invaluable in assessing the potential risks of different options and informing difficult decisions. This is not to argue that social work skills will become mechanistic or that casework will be reduced to a bureaucratic form of case management, but simply that evidence-based practice will require an ability to weigh up and evaluate whatever supporting evidence is available.

Conclusion

This book has explored the circumstances of very young children who spend extensive periods in care and accommodation in England and Wales. It has demonstrated the close relationship between parental problems such as drug and alcohol abuse, mental ill health and domestic violence, their current management and children's well-being. It has traced the extent of loss and change in the lives of even very young children, and identified an intricate relationship between parents' problems, constant change both outside and within the care system and delays in making difficult and complex decisions. An important finding has been how difficult it is for concerned professionals to keep the needs of the child at the heart of decision-making, and not be deflected by all the many other pressures demanding to be taken into account.

The children who formed the focus of this book had all become looked after between 1996 and 1997, five or six years before the study was complete. Much of what we found out about them was retrospective, and interviewees were able to discuss whether changes were now in place to address some of the problems we identified. Major policy initiatives aimed at reducing instability and delay in the care system, improving arrangements for adoption and delivering better outcomes for all children, including those most vulnerable, had been introduced in the intervening period. Evidence from the national statistics was supported by the accounts of practitioners and their managers, all of which suggested that the experiences of very young children coming into care might be a little more positive today. This was supported by findings from a second cohort of children who had entered the care of the same authorities about two and a half years later than those whose experiences are discussed in this book.

Nevertheless we also identified a number of areas that still need to be addressed. While there may be improvements to stability in the care system, children still move placements too frequently. The rate and reasons for moves need to be continuously monitored – as do the characteristics of children who change placements: some of the very young children in this study moved as frequently as did the teenagers in the full cohort (Ward 2004). Similarly, although there is some evidence that fewer children have to wait for quite so long before achieving permanence, delays and their reasons still need to be carefully monitored.

The findings from the study discussed in this book indicate where practitioners might make better use of information about children's previous experiences and the organisation's past performance in order to improve evidence-based practice and inform decision-making. Before this objective can be achieved, more attention will need to be devoted to improving understanding of how parents' problems can impact on their children when there are inadequate protective measures in place, and of how repeated experience of change and loss can affect young children's ability to form attachments. The Integrated Children's System has the potential to support such activities, but training will need to address IT and analysis skills if it is to be used effectively. Any attempts to build on the findings from this book to make changes to policy, practice and training will, of course, be aimed at meeting the over-riding objective – to improve the quality of experience and therefore outcomes for this group of very young, very vulnerable children.

Supplementary Tables and Figure

Table A.1: *Health conditions of children at entry (n=15)*

Health condition	Number of cases
Drug withdrawal at birth	4
Foetal alcohol syndrome	2
Complex health needs following head injury	2
Cerebral palsy	1
Hearing impairment	1
Asthma	4
Eczema	1
Total	15

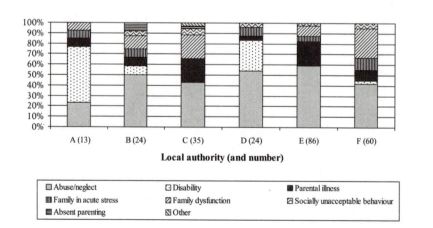

Figure A.1: Primary reasons for entry to care or accommodation (full cohort: n=242)

Table A.2: Child protection registrations

	Count (n=42)	Percentage
Neglect	12	29
Physical abuse	14	33
Emotional abuse	2	5
Combination	9	21
Not on register	5	12
Total	42	100

Table A.3: Age at exit by total number of addresses

	Total number of domiciles (n=36)				
Age at exit (months)	3 or less	4–6	7–9	10 or more	Total
15–18	1	4	1	0	6
19–24	1	0	2	1	4
25–30	1	3	3	2	9
31–36	1	1	0	1	3
37–48	2	1	5	1	9
49 or more	1	1	1	2	5
Total	7	10	12	7	36

Three of the sample of 42 children still looked after, three with missing data.

Table A.4: Strengths and Difficulties Questionnaire (n=6)

SDQ subscale	Banding		
	Normal	Borderline or abnormal	Total
Emotional symptoms	5	1	6
Conduct problems	3	3	6
Hyperactivity	3	3	6
Peer problems	6	0	6
Pro-social behaviour	6	0	6

Table A.5: Months from entry to best interests decision

Entry to best interests decision (months)	Count (n=21)	Percentage
5 or less	6	29
6–12	9	43
13–18	3	14
>18	3	14
Total	21	100

References

Abel, E.L. (1997) 'Maternal alcohol consumption and spontaneous abortion.' *Alcohol and Alcoholism 32*, 3, 211–219.

Adoption Act (1976) London: HMSO.

Adoption Agencies and Children (Arrangements for Placement and Review. (Miscellaneous Amendments) Regulations (1997) London: HMSO.

Adoption Agency Regulations (1983) London: HMSO.

Adoption (Amendment) Rules (1991) London: HMSO.

Adoption and Children Act (2002) London: HMSO.

Adoption Rules (1984) London: HMSO.

Ainsworth, M.D.S. (1989) 'Attachments beyond infancy.' *American Psychologist 44*, 4, 709–716.

Ainsworth, M.D.S., Blehar, M.C., Waters, E. and Wall, S. (1978) *Patterns of Attachment: A Psychological Study of the Strange Situation.* Hillsdale, NJ: Lawrence Erlbaum.

Aldridge, J. and Becker, S. (2003) *Children Caring for Parents with Mental Illness: Perspectives of Young Carers, Parents and Professionals.* Bristol: The Policy Press.

BAAF and the Fostering Network (2005) *The Cost of Foster Care.* London: British Association for Adoption and Fostering.

Bebbington, A. and Miles, J. (1989) 'The background of children who enter local authority care.' *British Journal of Social Work 19*, 349–368.

Beckett, C. (2000) 'Waiting for court decisions.' *Adoption and Fostering 24*, 2, 55–62.

Beckett, C. (2001) 'The wait gets longer: An analysis of recent information on court delays.' *Adoption and Fostering 25*, 4, 60–67.

Beckett, C. and McKeigue, B. (2003) 'Children in limbo: Cases where court cases have taken two years or more.' *Adoption and Fostering 27*, 3, 31–40.

Berridge, D. (1999) 'Child welfare in England: Problems, promises and prospects.' *International Journal of Social Work 8*, 4, 288–296.

Biehal, N., Clayden, J., Stein, M. and Wade, J. (1995) *Moving On: Young People and Leaving Care Schemes.* London: The Stationery Office.

Bowlby, J. (1979) *The Making and Breaking of Affectional Bonds.* New York: Routledge.

Bremner, J.G. (1991) *Infancy.* Oxford: Blackwell.

Brodzinsky, D., Schecter, D., Braff, A., and Singer, L. (1984) 'Psychological and academic adjustment in adopted children.' *Journal of Consulting and Clinical Psychology 52*, 582–590.

Budgell, R., Clare, M., Noolan, J. and Robertson, L. (in press) 'Promoting the health and well being of indigenous minority children in Canada and Australia.' In J. Scott and H. Ward (eds) *Safeguarding and Promoting the Well Being of Children, Families and their Communities.* London: Jessica Kingsley Publishers.

Carr-Hill, R., Dixon, P., Mannion, R., Rice, N., Rudat, K., Sinclair, R. and Smith, P. (1997) *A Model of the Determinants of Expenditure on Children's Personal Social Services.* York: University of York.

Children Act (1975) London: HMSO.

Children Act (1989) London: HMSO.

Children Act (2004) London: HMSO.

Choice Protects (2003) *Stability in Foster Care.* Seminar held at the Royal Academy of Engineering, Westminster, 22–23 January 2003. www.dfes.gov.uk/choiceprotects/publications/

Christoffersen, M.N. (1996) 'A follow-up study of out-of-home care in Denmark: Long-term effects on self-esteem among abused and neglected children.' *International Journal of Child and Family Welfare 1*, 1, 25–39.

Clapton, G. (2003) *Birth Fathers and their Adoption Experiences.* London: Jessica Kingsley Publishers.

Cleaver, H. (2000) *Fostering Family Contact: A Study of Children, Parents and Foster Carers.* London: The Stationery Office.

Cleaver, H. and Freeman, P. (1995) *Parental Perspectives in Cases of Suspected Child Abuse.* London: HMSO.

Cleaver, H., Unell, I. and Aldgate, J. (1999) *Children's Needs – Parenting Capacity.* London: The Stationery Office.

Cleaver, H. and Walker, S. with Meadows, P. (2004) *Assessing Children's Needs and Circumstances: The Impact of the Assessment Framework.* London: Jessica Kingsley Publishers.

Cleaver, H., Ward, H., Pithouse, A., Rose, W., Scott, J. and Walker, S. (forthcoming) *A Pilot Study to Assess the Development of a Multi-agency and Integrated Approach to the Delivery of Services to Children and their Families*; Report to Funders. London: Royal Holloway, University of London.

Cooper, A. and Webb, L. (1999) 'Out of the maze: Permanency planning in a postmodern world.' *Journal of Social Work Practice 13*, 2, 119–134.

Courtney, M.E., Piliavin, I., Grogan-Kaylor, A. and Nesmith, A. (2001) 'Foster youth transitions to adulthood: A longitudinal view of youth leaving care.' *Child Welfare 80.* 6, 685–717.

Courtney, M., Terao, S. and Bost, N. (2004) *Midwest Evaluation of the Adult Functioning of Former Foster Youth: Conditions of Youth Preparing to Leave State Care.* Chicago, IL: Chapin Hall Centre for Children, University of Chicago.

Cousins, W., Montieth, M., Larkin, E. and Percy, A. (2003) *The Care Careers of Younger Looked After Children: Findings from the Multiple Placements Project.* Belfast: Institute of Child Care Research.

Crittenden, P.M. (1995) 'Attachment and psychopathology'. In S. Goldberg, R. Muir and J. Kerr (eds) *Attachment Theory: Social, Developmental and Clinical Perspectives.* Hillsdale, NJ: The Analytic Press.

Department for Education and Skills (2003) *Children's Social Services Core Information Requirements: Process Model.* London: Department for Education and Skills.

Department for Education and Skills (2004a) *Every Child Matters: Change for Children.* London: The Stationery Office.

Department for Education and Skills (2004b) *The Children Act Report 2003.* London: The Stationery Office.

Department for Education and Skills (2005a) *Statistics of Education: Outcome Indicators for Looked after Children. Twelve Months to 30 September 2004.* London: HMSO.

Department for Education and Skills (2005b) *Statistics of Education: Children Looked After by Local Authorities Year Ending 31 March 2004, Volume 1: Commentary and National Tables.* London: HMSO.

Department for Education and Skills (2005c) *The Integrated Children's System: A Statement of Business Requirements (LAC (2005) 3).* London: Department for Education and Skills.

Department of Health (1990) *Children Act 1989 Guide to Principles and Practice.* London: The Stationery Office.

Department of Health (1991) *The Children Act Guidance and Regulations. Volume Three: Family Placements.* London: The Stationery Office.

Department of Health (1998a) *Someone Else's Children. Inspections of Planning and Decision Making for Children Looked After and the Safety of Children Looked After.* London: The Stationery Office.

Department of Health (1998b) *Modernising Social Services: Promoting Independence, Improving Protection, Raising Standards.* Cm. 4169. London: The Stationery Office.

Department of Health (1999a) *The Government's Objectives for Children's Social Services.* London: Department of Health.

Department of Health (1999b) *The Personal Social Services Performance Assessment Framework.* London: Department of Health.

Department of Health (1999c) *Adoption Now; Messages from Research.* Chichester: John Wiley & Sons Ltd.

Department of Health (2000a) *Prime Minister's Review of Adoption: Report from the Performance and Innovation Unit.* London: Department of Health.

Department of Health (2000b) *Adoption: A New Approach.* White Paper. London: The Stationery Office.

Department of Health (2000c) *Integrated Children's System: Briefing Paper No. 1.* London: Department of Health.

Department of Health (2001a) *Developing Quality to Protect Children.* London: Department of Health.

Department of Health (2001b) *National Adoption Standards.* London: Department of Health.

Department of Health (2002) *Improvement, Expansion and Reform: The Next Three Years Priorities and Planning Framework 2003–2006.* London: Department of Health.

Department of Health, Department for Education and Employment and Home Office (2000) *Framework for the Assessment of Children in Need and their Families.* London: The Stationery Office.

Department of Health, Home Office, Department for Education and Employment and National Assembly for Wales (1999) *Working Together to Safeguard Children: A Guide to Interagency Working to Safeguard and Promote the Welfare of Children* (consultation draft). London: Department of Health.

Dixon, J. and Stein, M. (2002) *Still a Bairn: Throughcare and Aftercare Services in Scotland.* Edinburgh: The Scottish Executive.

Falkov, A. (2002) 'Addressing family needs when a parent is mentally ill.' In H. Ward and W. Rose (eds) *Approaches to Needs Assessment in Children's Services.* London: Jessica Kingsley Publishers.

Family Justice Council (2004) Minutes of the conference held at the Radisson Edwardian Grafton Hotel on Thursday 7 and Friday 8 October.

Fratter, J., Rowe, J., Stapsford, D. and Thoburn, J. (1991) *Permanent Family Placement: A Decade of Experience.* London: British Association for Adoption and Fostering.

Gatehouse, M., Statham, J. and Ward, H. (2004) *The Knowledge: How to Get the Information You Need Out of Your Computers and Information Systems. A Practical Guide for Children's Social Services.* London: Institute of Education.

Gatehouse, M. and Ward, H. (2003) *Making Use of Information in Children's Social Services. Final Report to the Welsh Office of Research and Development for Health and Social Care.* Loughborough: Centre for Child and Family Research.

Goodman, R. (1997) 'The strengths and difficulties questionnaire: A research note.' *Journal of Child Psychology and Allied Disciplines 38,* 5, 581–586.

Goodman, R., Meltzer, H. and Bailey, V. (1998) 'The strengths and difficulties questionnaire: A pilot study on the validity of the self-report version.' *European Child and Adolescent Psychiatry 7,* 125–130.

Hartnett, M., Falconnier, L., Leathers, S. and Testa, M. (1999) *Placement Stability Study.* Chicago: University of Illinois.

Harwin, J., Owen, M., Locke, R. and Forrester, D. (2001) *Making Care Orders Work: A Study of Care Plans and their Implementation.* London: The Stationery Office.

HM Government (2003) *Every Child Matters.* Green Paper, Cm.5860. London: Department for Education and Skills.

Howe, D. (2001) 'Age at placement, adoption experience and adult adopted people's contact with their adoptive and birth mothers: An attachment perspective.' *Attachment and Human Development 3,* 2, 222–237.

Howe, D., Brandon, M., Hinings, D. and Schofield, G. (1999) *Attachment Theory, Child Maltreatment and Family Support.* Basingstoke: Macmillan.

Howe, D., Shemmings, D. and Feast, J. (2001) 'Age at placement and adult adopted people's experience of being adopted.' *Child & Family Social Work 6,* 4, 337–349.

Human Rights Act (1998) London: The Stationery Office.

Hunt, G. (1998) *Whistle-blowing in the Social Services. Public Accountability and Professional Practice.* London: Edward Arnold.

Ivaldi, G. (2000) *Surveying Adoption: A Comprehensive Analysis of Local Authority Adoptions 1998–1999 (England).* London: British Association for Adoption and Fostering.

Jackson, S. and Thomas, N. (1999) *On the Move Again? What Works in Creating Stability for Looked After Children.* Essex: Barnardos.

Jansen, M., Schuller, C., Johannes, H. and Arends, C. (1996) 'Outcome research in residential child care: Behavioural changes of treatment completers and treatment non-completers.' *International Journal of Child Welfare 1,* 1, 40–56.

Jones, D.P.H., Bentovim, A., Cameron, H., Vizard, E. and Wolkinel, S. (1991) 'Significant harm in context: The child psychiatrist's contribution.' In M. Adcock, R. White and A. Hollows (eds) *Significant Harm.* Croydon: Significant Publications.

Katz, L. (1990) 'Effective permanency planning for children in foster care. *Social Work 35,* 3.

Kearney, P., Levin, E. and Rosen, G. (2000) *Working with Families: Alcohol, Drug and Mental Health Problems.* London: National Institute of Social Work.

Kroll, B. and Taylor, A. (2003) *Parental Substance Misuse and Child Welfare.* London: Jessica Kingsley Publishers.

Kufeldt, K., Armstrong, J. and Dorosh, M. (1995) 'How children in care view their own and their foster families: A research study.' *Child Welfare 74,* 3, 695–715.

Kufeldt, K. and Stein, M. (2005) 'The voice of young people: Reflections on the process of leaving care and the care experience.' In J. Scott and H. Ward (eds) *Safeguarding and Promoting the Well-being of Children, Families and their Communities.* London: Jessica Kingsley Publishers.

Lamb, M. (1981) 'The development of social expectations in the first year of life.' In M.E. Lamb and L.R. Sherrods (eds) *Infant Social Cognition: Empirical and Theoretical Considerations.* Hillsdale, NJ: Lawrence Erlbaum.

Laming, Lord H. (2003) *The Victoria Climbié Inquiry.* London: The Stationery Office.

Lord Chancellor's Department (2002a) *Scoping Study on Delay in Children Act Cases.* London: The Stationery Office.

Lord Chancellor's Department (2002b) *Draft Protocol on Judicial Case Management in Children's Act Cases.* London: The Stationery Office.

Lowe, N. and Murch, M. (2002) *The Plan for the Child: Adoption or Long-term Fostering.* London: British Association for Adoption and Fostering.

Main, M. (1995) 'Attachment theory, social development and clinical perspectives.' In S. Goldberg, R. Muir and J. Kerr (eds) *Attachment Theory: Social, Developmental and Clinical Perspectives.* Hillsdale, NJ: The Analytic Press.

Maluccio, A.N., Pine, B. and Warsh, R. (1996) 'Incorporating content on family reunification into the social work curriculum.' *Journal of Social Work Education 3,* 363–374.

Millham, S., Bullock, R., Hosie, K. and Haak, M. (1986) *Lost in Care: The Problems of Maintaining Links Between Children in Care and their Families.* Aldershot: Gower.

Minty, B. (1999) 'Annotation: Outcomes in long-term foster family care.' *Journal of Child Psychology and Psychiatry 40,* 7, 991–999.

Moe, V. (2002) *A Prospective Longitudinal Study of Children Prenataly Exposed to Drugs: Prediction and Developmental Outcome at Four and a Half Years.* Oslo: Department of Psychology, University of Oslo.

Moe, V. and Slinning, K. (2003) 'Prenatal drug exposure and the conceptualisation of long-term effects.' *Scandinavian Journal of Psychology 43,* 41–47.

Monck, E., Reynolds, J. and Wigfall, V. (2003) *The Role of Concurrent Planning – Making Permanent Placements for Very Young Children.* London: British Association for Adoption and Fostering.

Munro, E.R., Holmes, L. and Ward, H. (2005) 'Researching vulnerable groups: Ethical issues and the effective conduct of research in local authorities.' *British Journal of Social Work 35,* 7, 1023–1038.

O'Sullivan, T. (1999) *Decision Making in Social Research.* Basingstoke: Macmillan.

Packman, J. and Hall, C. (1998) *From Care to Accommodation: Support, Protection and Control in Child Care Services.* London: The Stationery Office.

Poirier, M.A., Chamberland, C. and Ward, H. (forthcoming) *Les interactions entre les adultes qui prennent soins d'un enfant place en famille d'accueil: une étude sur les pratiques quotidiennes de collaboration.* La Revue Internationale de l'Education Familiale: Recherches et Interventions.

Putallaz, M., Philip, R., Costanzo, C., Grimes, L. and Sherman D.M. (1998) 'Intergenerational continuities and their influences on children's social development.' *Social Development 7,* 3, 389–427.

Quinton, D., Rushton, A., Dance, C. and Mayes, D. (1998) *Joining New Families: A Study of Adoption and Fostering in Middle Childhood.* Chichester: John Wiley & Sons.

Quinton, D. and Rutter, M. (1988) *Parenting Breakdown: The Making and Breaking of Inter-generational Links.* Aldershot: Avebury.

Quinton, D., Rutter, M. and Gulliver, L. (1990) 'Continuities in psychiatric disorders from childhood to adulthood in the children of psychiatric patients.' In L. Robins and M. Rutter (eds) *Straight and Devious Pathways from Childhood to Adulthood.* New York: Cambridge University Press.

Reder, P. and Duncan, S. (1999) *Lost Innocents: A Follow-up Study of Fatal Child Abuse.* London: Routledge.

Robbins, D. (1999) *Mapping Quality Protects in Children's Social Services: An Evaluation of Local Responses to the Quality Protects Programme.* London: Department for Education and Skills.

Robbins, D. (2000) *Tracking Progress in Children's Services: An Evaluation of Local Responses to the Quality Protects Programme, Year Two.* London: Department of Health.

Robbins, D. (2001) *Transforming Children's Services: An Evaluation of Local Responses to the Quality Protects Programme, Year Three.* London: Department of Health.

Rowe, J. and Lambert, L. (1973) *Children Who Wait.* London: Association of British Adoption Agencies.

Rutter, M. and ERA Study Team (1998) 'Developmental catch-up and deficit following adoption after severe global early deprivation.' *Journal of Child Psychology & Psychiatry 39,* 4, 465–476.

Rutter, M., Quinton, D. and Hill, J. (1990) *Straight and Devious Pathways from Childhood to Adulthood.* Cambridge: Cambridge University Press.

Schofield, G. (2001) 'Resilience and family placement: A lifespan perspective.' *Adoption and Fostering 25,* 3, 6–19.

Schulman, I. and Behrman, R.E. (1993) 'Adoption: Overview and recommendations.' *The Future of Children: Adoption 3,* 1, 4–16.

Sellick, C., Thoburn, J. and Philpot, T. (2004) *What Works in Adoption and Fostering.* London: Barnardos.

Selwyn, J. and Sturgess, W. (2001) *International Overview of Adoption: Policy and Practice.* Bristol: School for Policy Studies.

Sinclair, I. (2005) *Fostering Now: Messages from Research.* London: Jessica Kingsley Publishers.

Sinclair, I. and Gibbs, I. (1998) *Children's Homes: A Study in Diversity.* Aldershot: Gower.

Sinclair, I., Wilson, K. and Gibbs, I. (2000) *Supporting Foster Placements. Report Two.* York: Social Work Research and Development Unit, University of York.

Sinclair, I., Wilson, K. and Gibbs, I. (2004) *Foster Placements: Why They Succeed and Why They Fail.* London: Jessica Kingsley Publishers.

Skuse, T., Macdonald, I. and Ward, H. (2001) *Looking After Children: Transforming Data into Management Information, Report of Longitudinal Study at 30.9.99. Third Interim Report to the Department of Health.* Loughborough: Centre for Child and Family Research.

Skuse, T. and Ward, H. (2003) *Outcomes for Looked After Children: Children's Views of Care and Accommodation. An Interim Draft Report for the Department of Health.* Loughborough: Centre for Child and Family Research.

Slinning, K. (2003) *A Prospective Longitudinal Study of Children Prenataly Exposed to Substances: With Special Emphasis on Attention and Self-regulation.* Oslo: Department of Psychology, University of Oslo.

Social Exclusion Unit (2003) *A Better Education for Children in Care.* London: HMSO.

Tannenbaum, L. and Forehand, R. (1994) 'Maternal depressive mood: The role of the father in preventing adolescent behaviour problems.' *Behaviour Research and Therapy 32,* 321–326.

Thoburn, J. (2002) 'Family placement services.' In D. McNeish *et al.* (eds) *What Works? Effective Social Care Services for Children and Families.* London: Open University Press/Barnardos.

Triseliotis, J. (2002) 'Long-term foster care or adoption?' *Child & Family Social Work 7,* 23–33.

Tunnard, J. (2002) *Parental Problem Drinking and its Impact on Children*. Dartington: Research in Practice.

Wall, N. (1997) 'The courts and child protection – the challenge of hybrid cases.' *Child and Family Law Quarterly 9*, 4, 345–357.

Ward, H. (2004) 'Working with managers to improve services: Changes in the role of research in social care.' *Child and Family Social Work 9*, 1, 13–25.

Ward, H. (forthcoming) *Separating Families: How the Origins of Current Child Welfare Policy and Practice Can Be Traced to the Nineteenth-century Child Rescue Movement*. London: Jessica Kingsley Publishers.

Ward, H., Holmes, L., Soper, J. and Olsen, R. (2004) *The Costs and Consequences of Different Types of Child Care. Report to the Department of Health*. Loughborough: Centre for Child and Family Research.

Ward, H., Munro, E.R. and Caulfield, L. (forthcoming b) *Protecting and Promoting the Well Being of Very Young Children: A Prospective Study of Babies in Need or at Risk of Significant Harm*. Loughborough: Centre for Child and Family Research.

Ward, H. and Skuse, T. (1999) *Looking After Children: Using Data as Management Information, Report from the First Year of Data Collection. Report to the Department of Health*. Totnes: Dartington Research Unit.

Ward, H. and Skuse, T. (2001) 'Performance targets and stability of placements for children long looked after away from home.' *Children and Society 15*, 1–14.

Ward, H., Wynn, A., Macdonald, I. and Skuse, T. (forthcoming a) *Exploring Similarities and Differences in the Needs of Care Populations. Report to the Department for Education and Skills*. Loughborough: Centre for Child and Family Research.

Waterhouse, S. and Brocklesbury, E. (1999) *Placement Choices for Children in Temporary Foster Care*. London: National Foster Care Association.

Weir, A. and Douglas, A. (1999) *Child Protection and Adult Mental Health: Conflict of Interests?* Oxford: Butterworth Heinemann.

Whelan, D. (2003) 'Using attachment theory when placing siblings in foster care.' *Child and Adolescent Social Work Journal 20*, 1, 21–36.

Williams, J. (2001) '1998 Human Rights Act: Social work's new benchmark.' *British Journal of Social Work 31*, 831–844.

Williams, J. (2004) 'Social work, liberty and law.' *British Journal of Social Work 34*, 1, 27–52.

Zeanah, C. and Emde, R. (1994) 'Attachment disorders in infancy and childhood.' In M. Rutter, E. Taylor and L. Hersov (eds) *Child and Adolescent Psychiatry: Modern Approaches*. Oxford: Blackwell Scientific Publishers.

Subject Index

Author Index